HOW TO COMPETE BEYOND THE 1980s

Recent Titles from QUORUM BOOKS

HOW TO COMPETE BEYOND THE 1980s

Perspectives from High-Performance Companies

CONFERENCE PROCEEDINGS

Sponsored by

Federal Reserve Bank of Atlanta

Q

Quorum Books
Westport, Connecticut • London, England

Library of Congress Cataloging in Publication Data

Main entry under title:

How to compete beyond the 1980s.

   Papers presented at a conference held in Atlanta, Ga.
in April 1984.
   Bibliography: p.
   Includes index.
   1. Industrial management—Congresses.   2. Industrial
management—United States—Congresses.   3. Industrial
management—Southern States—Congresses.   I. Federal
Reserve Bank of Atlanta.
HD29.H68   1985   658   84-22629
ISBN 0-89930-096-0 (lib. bdg.)

Library of Congress Catalog Card Number: 84-22629
ISBN: 0-89930-096-0

First published in 1985 by Quorum Books

Greenwood Press
A division of Congressional Information Service, Inc.
88 Post Road West, Westport, Connecticut 06881

Printed in the United States of America

10 9 8 7 6 5 4 3 2 1

Contents

Preface

What is that special something that elevates certain companies above the corporate crowd? We at the Federal Reserve Bank of Atlanta asked ourselves this question when we heard accounts of companies not only surviving the recent recessions but actually profiting during hard economic times. So, we read more.

We read all the available literature on the subject. We discussed the issue among ourselves and our acquaintances. Then we studied a number of high-performance companies and discovered what we believe to be the common threads tying these companies together in success. This study led us to sponsor the conference "How to Compete Beyond the 1980s: Perspectives from High-Performance Companies" and to produce this book based on the proceedings.

These common threads seemed to be of particular interest at the time the conference was held at the Atlanta Hilton Hotel in April 1984. Although the long-awaited economic recovery was well underway, foreign companies continued outproducing and undercutting American firms. This, of course, caused many business people to look to the federal government for help. But others, we noticed, were finding ways to compete without help—they were developing new strategies and using new techniques. We invited speakers from these "other" companies, the ones that succeeded despite adversity, to join with economists and authors in speaking at our conference.

Our two-day conference drew approximately 200 chief executive officers, academics, and journalists to hear the success stories of companies in traditional industries, nontraditional industries, and banking, as well as to gather observations from those who watch and measure success.

We hope that in reading this book you will find some, if not all, of the management techniques discussed to be of use. Of course, the speakers' opinions are their own and do not necessarily reflect the views of the Atlanta Fed or the Federal Reserve System.

About the Contributors

William N. Cox, as vice president and associate director of research at the Federal Reserve Bank of Atlanta, helped supervise the Bank's Research Department. In that position, he guided the staff's research in national monetary policy, the financial services industry, the payments system, and the southeastern economy. He left the Atlanta Fed in October 1984 to organize his own Atlanta-based company, providing management information services for depository institutions.

Gerald Eickhoff established Bank Earnings International Holdings Limited in 1983 after heading the in-house consulting staff of Citizens and Southern National Bank of Georgia. His firm designs programs and products to improve service and earnings for banks. He holds M.B.A.s in economics and finance from Georgia State University.

M. Kathryn Eickhoff is executive vice president of Townsend-Greenspan & Co., Inc., an economic consulting group based in New York, and is executive director of ECONALYST, which provides Townsend-Greenspan's economic services to clients over ADP Network Services' worldwide computing system. She performed many of the duties of Townsend-Greenspan's president, Alan Greenspan, while he served as chairman of the President's Council of Economic Advisers from 1974 to 1977.

Eugene Epstein is senior economist at the New York Stock Exchange and was the principal writer of the recent NYSE study, "People and Productivity: A Challenge to Corporate America." He has also contributed to two previous NYSE studies, "U.S. Economic Performance in a Global Perspective" and "Building a Better Future: Economic Choices for the 1980s." He has written other articles on the importance of innovation in boosting economic growth. He was a writer and consultant before joining the Exchange in 1977. His books include *Making Money in Commodities* and *Electric Power from the Wind*.

William A. Fickling, Jr., organized Charter Medical Corporation in 1969 as an international health company based in Macon, Georgia. It has grown to include more than 53 psychiatric, addictive disease, and general acute care hospitals. He served as president before he was named chairman and chief executive officer in 1979. He served on the Atlanta Fed's board of directors from 1978 through 1983. He was designated deputy chairman for 1978–1979 and chairman for 1980–1983.

Robert P. Forrestal took office in December 1983 as president of the Federal Reserve Bank of Atlanta, after serving as first vice president from 1979. He joined the Federal Reserve in 1964 as an attorney in the legal division of the Federal Reserve Board in Washington, following three years of private law practice. He was appointed vice president and general counsel to the Atlanta Fed in 1970, then became senior vice president in 1974. He received his education at All Hallows Institute and St. John's University. His law degree is from Georgetown University Law Center.

Mark C. Hollis is vice president of public affairs and public relations for Publix Super Markets, Inc., based in Lakeland, Florida. He started with Publix as a bag boy when he was 12 years old, and has since worked in many capacities, including stock clerk, produce manager, store manager, director of personnel, and director of warehousing and distribution. In May 1974, he was elected to the board of directors of Publix, an aggressive food retailer that installed its own automated teller machine system in 1982. He received a B.A. from Stetson University and a Master's degree from Michigan State University in food distribution.

Thomas H. Jacobsen was named senior executive vice president of finance and administration for Barnett Banks of Florida, Inc., in 1982. He joined Barnett Banks as vice president of support services. He was elected chief operating officer in 1976 then later president and chief executive officer, of Barnett's south Florida affiliate, the organization's largest. Prior to joining Barnett, he was with the First National Bank of Chicago.

Rosabeth Moss Kanter, whose newest book is *The Change Masters: Innovation for Productivity in the American Corporation*, is the author of several books, as well as more than 80 articles. She is a professor of sociology and organization and management at Yale University. She is also chairman of Goodmeasure, Inc., a management consulting firm she cofounded.

Alan M. Kantrow is associate editor of the *Harvard Business Review* and author of *Industrial Renaissance*. He has written articles on management expert Peter Drucker, on the management of technology, and on industrial competition. He received an A.B. and a Ph.D. in the history of American civilization from Harvard University.

Donald L. Koch, as senior vice president and director of research of the Federal Reserve Bank of Atlanta, was responsible for the Atlanta Fed's economic research and public information activities. He served as associate economist to the Federal Open Market Committee, the principal monetary policy body of the United States. He left the Atlanta Fed in April 1984 to join a securities firm in Atlanta.

Bernard Marcus has been chairman of the board and chief executive officer of the Home Depot since he helped create the Atlanta-based chain of southeastern home improvement retail stores. He formerly was chairman and president of Handy Dan Home Improvement Centers, which operated approximately 70 home improvement retail stores in the western United States. Before that, he served as executive vice president of Daylin, Inc., a publicly owned consumer merchandising and health services company.

Preston Martin is vice chairman of the Board of Governors of the Federal Reserve System. He is also chairman of the Bank Activities Committee and a member of the Group of Experts on Payments Systems, Bank for International Settlements in Basel, Switzerland. Prior to his appointment to the Board of Governors, he was senior advisor on housing to the Reagan Administration's Transition Task Force and chairman of the Taxation Task Force of President Reagan's Committee on Housing. He was chairman of the Federal Home Loan Bank Board from 1969 to 1972. He was a founder of the Federal Home Loan Mortgage Corporation and was also California Savings and Loan commissioner from 1967 to 1969.

Ken Millen is vice president of personnel at Management Science America (MSA) of Atlanta, the largest independent software supplier in the country. He previously served as MSA's director of personnel and was instrumental in building the college training and management development programs.

Marvin Runyon, as president of Nissan Motor Company's American subsidiary, Nissan U.S.A., has adapted the Japanese management techniques of the parent company to his Smyrna, Tennessee, plant. He worked for Ford Motor Company for 37 years, beginning as an hourly employee in an assembly plant in Dallas, Texas, then moving up to become manager for two assembly plants, general manager of the automobile assembly division, and vice president of the power-train and chassis operations. He received his B.S. degree in management engineering from Texas A&M.

John A. Savage is manager of personnel services for Nucor Corporation, a steel-making firm based in Charlotte, N.C., that has remained prosperous even in recent years that have been difficult for the American steel industry. Before joining Nucor, he was personnel manager for Avon Products in Newark, Delaware, and senior employee relations assistant for Mobil Oil Corporation in Paulsboro, New Jersey. He has written an article on Nucor in the *Personnel Administrator* and conducted a case study on the company for the Council for a Union-Free Environment.

Delores W. Steinhauser, as an economist at the Federal Reserve Bank of Atlanta, coordinated the development of the Research Department's regional data base and helped automate the department. She left the Atlanta Fed in June 1984 to join the management consulting services division of Coopers and Lybrand in New York City.

Robert Strickland has served as chairman of the board of Trust Company of Georgia since 1978. Trust Company is one of the founders of the new Cirrus nationwide network of shared automated teller machines. He was elected in 1976 as president of Trust Company, a bank he joined in 1948 as a management trainee. He is a past president of the Atlanta Chamber of Commerce and of the Georgia Bankers Association.

Joel R. Wells, Jr., is chairman of the board of Sun Banks, Inc., a Florida bank holding company. He was named president in 1976, then chief executive officer in 1982. He was elected to the board of Sun Bank, N.A. at the age of 32, making him the youngest director in the bank's history. Before joining Sun Banks, he was president of Major Realty Corporation. He received his B.S./B.A. degree in 1950 and his law degree in 1951.

C. Martin Wood III is senior vice president and chief financial officer of Flowers Industries, Inc., a Georgia-based baking company known for buying financially distressed bakeries and making them profitable. He joined Flowers Industries in 1970 as director of new product development. He has a degree from Princeton University and an M.B.A. from the University of Virginia's Colgate Darden School of Business Administration.

ROBERT P. FORRESTAL

Introductory Remarks

Novelist F. Scott Fitzgerald once observed that the rich are different from the rest of us. Ernest Hemingway supposedly replied, "Yes, they have more money."

At the Federal Reserve Bank of Atlanta, we have come to the conclusion that high-performance companies, too, are a lot like the rest—except that they possess a special something that elevates them above the corporate crowd. And that special something is more than money, although corporate performance often seems to produce profits.

Our intent during this conference is to look at some of the Southeast's most successful companies and try to identify the elements that set them apart. What is the chemistry—or is it alchemy?—of the high-performance company, or, for that matter, of the high-performance organization or institution?

The dual thrust of our investigation should be apparent from the title we chose for this conference: "How to Compete Beyond the 1980s: Perspectives from High-Performance Companies." We have invited chief executives of several successful corporations to tell us their stories, so we can consider how other companies can adopt or adapt certain ideas or philosophies to their own operations.

Why does the Federal Reserve Bank of Atlanta, a unit of our nation's central bank, care about such things? Let me try to explain.

We feel it is crucial that we find the keys that can unlock our nation's creativity and productivity. What has happened to the economic magic we used to describe as "America's industrial miracle"? Many of us wonder. Our productivity gains have failed to keep pace with those of some of our trading partners, notably Japan. That nation's economic successes have been chronicled frequently in recent years, and we respect those achievements. But do we have to step aside for Japan or anyone else? I think not, and I hope you will agree when you have heard from our panel of experts.

We happen to believe that our national revival must come, not from sweeping federal initiatives or edicts, but from the imagination and efforts of individual corporations and institutions.

The Atlanta Fed's interest in reviving national productivity is not a new development. It took embryonic form during the recession years of 1981 and 1982, when our economists noted that some companies seemed to prosper even during the worst of times. Our curiosity led us to a major conference in March 1983 that featured such experts as futurist Alvin Toffler; Robert Waterman, Jr., co-author of *In Search of Excellence*, which still ranks high on the best-seller lists; and Arthur Levitt, Jr., chairman of the American Stock Exchange.

More recently, our Research Department has conducted a major study of high-performance companies, which will be described during this conference. A more detailed report on the findings of that study will be carried in the April 1984 issue of the Atlanta Fed's monthly magazine, the *Economic Review*.

Before we get underway, let me give special thanks to William N. Cox, Katherine Hart, Bobbie McCrackin, and Delores Steinhauser of the Atlanta Fed's Research Department, who conducted that study. I'd also like to thank Carolyn Vincent, coordinator for this conference, and Donald Bedwell and Melinda Dingler, editors of these proceedings.

Our study of high-performance companies was guided by Donald L. Koch, the Atlanta Fed's director of research. He will provide an overview of the conference and detail some of the objectives that we hope to accomplish.

DONALD L. KOCH

Conference Purpose and Overview

How can we compete in the 1980s and beyond? What's all this folderol about how the Japanese can produce widgets better than we can? Bob Forrestal alluded to some of this nation's economic troubles that suggest a need for greater emphasis on superior, top-quality management. The evidence of that need is compelling, indicating that we must learn what we can from our most successful American corporations, if we are to regain our global competitiveness.

The Federal Reserve Bank of Atlanta started thinking a year ago about the lessons we might learn from high-performance companies. Our interest was whetted by our own research into high-technology companies in the Southeast, which turned up evidence that firms widely divergent in many ways share certain common traits that may contribute to their success. At the same time, we were intrigued by such thought-provoking books on management as *In Search of Excellence* and *The Change Masters*.

Our Atlanta Fed Research Department decided then to look at what the companies in our region were doing to compete effectively. We decided to look at the international economy to determine for ourselves the status of the United States compared with our trading partners.

We observed that the nations we trade with tend to be more concerned than we are about shipping their exports to other countries. The rest of the world places a higher priority on making sure the goods and services they make are bought by others. We, as a nation, experienced a net decline from 1965 to 1983 in exports as a percentage of the entire world economy. Over that same period, the less developed countries experienced an increase. Our noncompetitiveness is underscored by the fact that we have a sharp trade deficit—the gloomy prospect of a $100 billion deficit this year. That means we are importing far more Sonys, Danish furniture, and Mercedes automobiles than we are shipping such diverse goods as missiles and grain.

We're all familiar with the sharp inroads apparel imports have made.

We also know how foreign steel has penetrated world markets and we know about the auto sector. We are also aware how foreign competitors have penetrated our domestic electronics markets. If you walk through your house or your apartment, you can confirm the extent of that penetration pretty quickly. Did you know that virtually all the black-and-white television sets, three-quarters of the stereo equipment, more than half the radios, and nearly half the color televisions come from some other country?

Unfortunately, it doesn't end there. At the Atlanta Fed, we came to the conclusion that we were also losing some of the real proprietary leadership we've enjoyed in the past. We grew concerned that we also face world-class competition in such industries as commercial aircraft, industries that we used to call our own. Such industries that were once the exclusive domain of the United States are being lost to consortiums from other countries. Today, for instance, even major American air carriers are ordering jetliners like the European A-300.

Will computers be the next industry to vanish overseas? We've seen what the Japanese have done in the television market. And, in the terms of raw electronics, there isn't much difference between what's inside a color television set and what's in a computer. In fact, the value in parts is higher in televisions than in microcomputers.

When we looked at trends and productivity, we found we weren't improving our productivity vis-à-vis the countries with which we trade. The other countries were showing a sharp increase in both technology and human labor, in terms of increasing input per man-hour. At best, we were achieving less than four times the growth of our nearest competitor among the large industrial countries.

At the opposite pole, our savings rate ranks as one of the lowest among the industrialized nations—rather embarrassing for the society that produced Benjamin Franklin and a widely touted dedication to thrift. Unless we generate savings, we won't have capital available to invest. And without investment, we won't have the renewal factor so vital for the American economy to survive.

Look at the areas where we are supposed to be making a major commitment to the future. I refer to the labor-saving devices of the 1990s and beyond, such as industrial robotics. We can claim only 12 percent of the world's robots in service, while the Japanese have 67 percent. Neither do we match the commitment of other countries to industrial renewal and science. What about education? We do enjoy technological dominance in our schools and universities, but our engineering programs lag. The number of graduate engineers in our country, for instance, trails far behind the number in Japan.

More bad news? Unemployment, though continuing to edge downward as the recession fades into history, still remains high with nearly nine million Americans out of work. And although inflation has slowed dramatically over the past couple of years, it still remains high by historical standards and is like a sleeping dragon ready to rouse at any time.

Our working-age population promises to be another serious problem for our competitiveness as we go into the 1990s, because the bulk of our population, the "baby boomers," is growing older. The number of prime, high-energy-level people aged 25 to 34—the people who are the new focus of renewal and growth in our society—is expected to decline in the next 10 years. That means the people side of the equation, our real "soft assets," will be at an extraordinarily high premium.

Looking into these problems, we found that experts from various disciplines offer conflicting explanations for the serious erosion of the American dream. One group of professionals argues that the solution to the nation's problems has to do with macroeconomic external policies— monetary policy, fiscal policy, trade policy, and industrial policy—which means redeploying money and wealth to rebuild such "rust bowl" cities as Cleveland and Buffalo.

Another group of scholars says the real problem is culture, tradition, and behavioral ethics. They say we don't have the same number of children in the Boy Scouts as we did 20 years ago, that we have lost the commitment to the value structure and to the hard work that made this nation great. Instead, they say, we have become a consumptive society, using up our resources faster than we can restore them.

A group of securities analysts and financial specialists, on the other hand, contends that the real issue has to do with facility locational decisions and capital investment. Are we locating our plants in the Southeast or putting them in the Northeast or the Midwest? Are we maximizing the financial balance sheet to achieve the leverage we need in order to perform?

These experts say the issue is management selection. How do we choose the right people to lead? Do we need a new management matrix? Do we work in a hierarchal structure, or do we work in a cooperative, collegial structure?

How do we improve productivity through people if people are the salvation for the 1990s? What kind of people systems do we have in place or should we introduce if we want to overcome the inertia, the low productivity that we face as a nation?

Do we have the optimum culture for change? The answer lies in the synergistic understanding of what each discipline says. We have found that scholars and other "experts" do not tend to talk to each other. We seem to lack teamwork.

How do we as a nation address our problems and find solutions? Can we resolve our problems by tinkering with monetary and fiscal policy, with trade policy, with industrial policy—the various structural approaches that come under the heading of macroeconomic policy? Or are the solutions "micro"—can they be achieved on the factory floor and in our corporate offices rather than on Capitol Hill?

Our research turned up persuasive evidence that the latter comes closer to the mark—that micro solutions offer our greatest hope. We think some of the best evidence may be found in small, growth-oriented companies in which the entrepreneurial spirit flourishes—the kind of businesses that have created most of this nation's new jobs in recent years. But you can decide for yourself as you consider the experiences of corporate executives who will explain how their firms tackled problems and capitalized on opportunities.

Over the past six months, our Research Department has looked at companies in the Southeast to find those with a record of excellence. We felt that if we could identify companies that are doing things right—not only in establishing a history of impressive earnings, but also in managing their people—they might well serve as a model that other American companies could follow, to the benefit of our nation's productivity.

But how do you go about finding what we call "high-performance" companies? The 44 men and women who serve as directors of the Atlanta Fed and its five branches—in Birmingham, Jacksonville, Miami, Nashville, and New Orleans—provided a good nucleus for our investigation. These directors, mostly business people from throughout our six-state District, have a sensitive feel for the pulse of their communities and the companies with a record of superb performance. They helped us to identify some of those companies. Securities analysts and others who watch industrial performance offered their perspectives on those companies and suggested their own nominees. These companies ranged from traditional firms to high-tech newcomers, from textiles to microprocessors, from airlines to bakeries. And they varied in age from a mere four or five years to more than 100 years.

After we had assembled our list of corporate nominees, our economists performed quantitative data work to screen their financial performance. Some companies, of course, didn't measure up to their billing. And, finally, when we had drawn up a list of southeastern companies that looked good on paper, we went in with a team of four or five analysts and spent a day and a half with their managements to see if they lived up to expectations. We found that some companies with impressive financial results didn't show up well in their "people" relations, or they fell short in other ways. They were bureaucratic, for instance, plagued by "turf battles," or they tended to look upon their employees as commodities rather than as assets.

When we found a company with overall high performance, we zeroed in to detect its secrets of success, trying to determine what its management did that others did not do.

We came up with an acronym summarizing the characteristics we found in 22 premier southeastern companies we identified and interviewed. We call it the "TEAM" approach to management. This stands for technology, entrepreneurship, allegiance, and marketing.

Well-managed companies, we found, tend to be technologically focused, and they use technology as a major offensive weapon rather than as a defensive one. These companies beat the competition time and time again.

The superior companies also respect the entrepreneur. They attend to detail and seek two-way communication between management and staff. They tend to be lean, with few levels of management. At least two companies we visited functioned with only five management levels from the CEO to the bottom line worker.

These successful companies work to establish congruent goals and to give employees a direct identification with the purposes of the organization. Their employees think about the company in their off-hours and give that company the best 50 to 60 hours in their week. Other characteristics? These companies are decentralized, autonomous, informal, and they avoid singling out executives for "perks," such as special automobiles or dining rooms.

We found a high degree of allegiance among employees in the high-performance companies. They share a family feeling and a great commitment to perform. Incentives are tied to results because these firms are results-based organizations with an emphasis on training, freedom for employees to voice opinions candidly, and a recognition throughout the organization that long-term employees are the company's most valuable assets.

Other characteristics include a focus on market strategy and an emphasis on corporate "niching" or high value-added products. These firms like to be market leaders. They stick to what they know best and back that with long-term orientation; they look far beyond impressive quarterly earnings.

Surprisingly, each of the high-performance companies we studied seems to have an altruistic bent. They want to serve mankind in some way. They want a corporate commitment that extends beyond the profit motive.

The people who worked on our study for six months were thrilled about coming to grips with the real questions of management excellence. We found companies that ignored strategies considered fundamental by some of the recent books on corporate excellence. And we found contradictions, sometimes within fine companies themselves. Still, at the end of our study we agreed on a series of conclusions that might at least point the way toward answers for the future.

We have promised to share with you some of the fruits of our research—the stories of high-performance companies and their secrets of success. We hope to bring you perspectives not only from individual companies, but from those who watch and measure their success. We'll try to find out what these companies do that makes them rise above the competition. We'll present both the specific strategies that some of these companies use to compete and the broader perspective from economists and securities experts.

You'll receive some tips from the executives of three growth companies: Ken Millen of Management Science America, who will tell us why "People Are the Key to Success"; Bernard Marcus of The Home Depot, who will explain why his firm emphasizes education for managers and employees; and William A. Fickling, Jr., of Charter Medical Corporation, who will encourage us to succeed by anticipating trends.

We'll also find out how certain imaginative companies are revitalizing traditional industries when we hear Marvin Runyon of Nissan U.S.A., C. Martin Wood III of Flowers Industries, and Mark C. Hollis of Publix Super Markets.

Three top southeastern bankers will offer us their insights: Robert Strickland of Trust Company of Georgia, Joel R. Wells, Jr., of Sun Banks, and Thomas H. Jacobsen of Barnett Banks of Florida. Another perspective on banking will be offered by consultant Gerald Eickhoff of Bank Earnings International.

Two experts in management studies—Alan M. Kantrow of the *Harvard Business Review* and Rosabeth Moss Kanter, author of *The Change Masters: Innovation for Productivity in the American Corporation*—will help us understand how companies can stimulate innovation in a changing environment.

Preston Martin, vice chairman of the Board of Governors of the Federal Reserve System, will focus on "Innovation, Motivation, and Monetary Policy." Then we'll be offered a Wall Street viewpoint from Eugene Epstein of the New York Stock Exchange.

Leading off will be M. Kathryn Eickhoff, executive vice president of Townsend-Greenspan, an economic consulting firm, and executive director of ECONALYST, which provides Townsend-Greenspan's economic services to clients.

HOW TO COMPETE BEYOND THE 1980s

M. KATHRYN EICKHOFF

Hail! Seekers of the Golden Fleece

In a free-enterprise system, the role of profits and their economic importance should be self-evident. However, instead of profit seeking being viewed as a virtuous pursuit of which one should be proud, it is often considered as, at best, an embarrassment. We speak of monopoly profits, of excess profits, even of obscene profits, but rarely do we listen with awe and admiration to heroic stories of the difficulties encountered in achieving an additional 1 percent return on investment.

Profits perform many important functions in our economy. Most important, they provide the incentive to individuals to take the risks and make the decisions that keep our economy vital. They are the "golden fleece" for which our enterprises must strive. A vital, growing economy is something we all want. Although we read about the profits (and losses) of large companies, smaller companies are often more motivated by profits. The high-performance, small- to medium-sized company, with its ability to double or triple in size overnight, is a source of great vitality to the economy.

Economists often view profits as the residual income share. While this is not a glamorous view, it identifies an important social function played by profits. Profits buffer or protect other economic participants from the vicissitudes of the business cycle. When the economy contracts, profits drop far more than employment or rental income. In a recovery, profits may soar, particularly if a company improved its efficiency during the recession.

What's more, profits are the rewards for risk taking. Industries with inherently more risk receive a greater reward for success. Companies in such industries must earn an above-average return to stay in business and to attract investors when additional capital is required. The biggest profits go to those who see a way to avoid or conquer the risks others perceive as deterrents.

Profits are also the way the market makes its preferences known. They are the main mechanisms for allocating resources in our economy. If too high a profit is earned—too high by the standards of other entrepreneurs willing and able to compete for a lower return—new businesses will enter the market. If returns are too low, some companies will be forced out.

Finally, profits constitute the primary source of savings and investment. Investment has always been necessary for the survival of mankind. Unless seed is saved, next year's harvest cannot be planted. Even as a hunter, ancient man learned to set aside portions of a kill in order to make tools and weapons. Times have changed, but this remains the same.

If we make no attempt to invest, our factories and tools will decay. We must set aside at least enough to replace existing facilities as they wear out. But unless we have a purely static society—with the same population, the same wants, and the same needs—even replacement cost depreciation cannot prevent us from slipping backward to an ever-lower standard of living. This is not our goal; most people want to move ahead to a higher standard of living. To do this, we must invest in the future. To obtain the wherewithal to invest, we must save.

In some societies, individuals save significant portions of their incomes, contributing to a rapid investment rate in their economies. The Japanese, for example, save over 20 percent of their disposable income. Throughout history, the Chinese savings rate has been far higher than that of other cultures in Southeast Asia. When the Chinese have emigrated to other countries, they have quickly become a major factor in the economic life of their new homelands.

In contrast, since World War II, our personal savings rate generally has ranged between 5 percent and 8 percent. Currently it is close to 5 percent, significantly lower than a decade ago. Furthermore, our government is a substantial net dissaver. With the federal deficit at nearly $200 billion this year and likely to climb to $350 billion before 1990 if nothing is done, the federal government consumes far more than individuals, in total, save. Since the federal deficit does not contribute directly to investment, with rare exception, profits (including depreciation) are the primary source of funds for new investment.

Corporations have a high savings rate. Besides depreciation, they generally save or retain more than half of every dollar of profit. In addition, individuals and institutions receiving dividends from companies tend to save more than individuals receiving primarily wage income. Unfortunately, profits as a share of total income have declined at the same time government has preempted a larger share of available savings. Profit margins, which ran 13–14 percent in the 1960s, are now less than 9 percent after a year of rapid recovery.

As profit margins eroded in the 1970s, inflation introduced great uncertainty into the economic outlook. As a result, required rates of return on investment began to climb. Capital investment is hierarchical in nature. Many projects might produce a 1 or 2 percent return, but few will yield 30 percent or more. As inflation drove interest rates up, they became a reason to require a higher rate of return. When you drive up hurdle rates, you suppress the total amount of investment and you change the types of investments made. Projects requiring a long-term commitment to an industry, locality, or product become less desirable than investments with a quick payoff and a high discounted cash flow. The increase in hurdle rates was not unreasonable in our situation. In an era with little stability in crucial parameters more than a year or two out, it would be imprudent to undertake projects requiring 20, 30, or 40 years to recover the investment. Cost-reduction projects tend to take precedence over plant expansion.

That is what is happening currently. The latest Department of Commerce survey reports that nonfarm businesses plan to increase their plant and equipment expenditures nearly 14 percent in 1984, but almost all of the increase will go for equipment. Investment in industrial buildings in constant dollars has been in a declining trend since the late 1960s. The investments occurring today are from a backlog of cost-cutting measures held back by three years of recession. Furthermore, our surveys do not report on the extent of "disinvestment"—on how many facilities are being closed or sold.

Two revealing articles appeared recently in *The Wall Street Journal*. On the front page was a story on medium-sized towns in the Midwest still in the throes of the recession because of lost industry and their farmers' problems. Typically, the loss of a major employer leads to reduced business downtown, which leads to a further loss of jobs in retailing. These developments reflect the failure of the core companies in these communities to make the investments to keep them competitive.

Meanwhile, the back section of the paper carried a story on the efforts of large companies to reduce their break-even point by closing facilities. Such efforts were reported as necessary to restore profitability and ensure the survival of the companies during the next downturn. No connection was made between the two stories, but there is an important link. Many of the plants being closed were in the same medium-sized communities whose plight was being lamented on page one. Had the profits been there, had inflation not pushed hurdle rates up, companies might have invested in facilities that would have kept these communities competitive today.

Is it any wonder that we are viewed as incapable of competing in world markets? For a decade, many of our major industries have engaged in little more than maintenance and repair, while other parts of the world have been building modern facilities.

The owners of a new manufacturing facility, which I toured recently, have gathered state-of-the-art technology from around the world for every stage of the production process. Robots are used in hazardous areas such as painting, and a computer record follows the product from the moment it starts down the assembly line until the last warranty expires. Suppliers have been encouraged to locate facilities near the plant to reduce delivery time. In fact, there is little provision for storing parts at the plant. The assembly line begins only a few feet from the receiving dock. Compared with the traditional American assembly line operation, this one seems to have revolutionized everything, including personnel policies.

The people manning the various steps in the production process are organized into teams with two assignments: to get the job done and to figure out how to do it better. In their view, they will be able to compete effectively only if they can improve their product 3 percent or more each year, either by better quality or lower cost. Each team is designed to be nearly self-sufficient and to work out its own problems. There are no foremen or supervisors, but there is a plant manager. I was surprised at one point to find three workers sitting apart. They explained that sometimes automation does not work as planned. A machine was creating a small burr on one part. Their team had found they could solve the problem temporarily by using a hand file to remove the burr. This gave another group time to solve the problem with the machine.

I talked with the people working on the teams. They came to this plant from many fields, including more traditional manufacturing firms, but they had no special skills. With the exception of one man who lamented that there is "no one to tell you what to do," the employees support the program. Reputedly, the facility is the world's lowest cost producer of diesel engines. It is not in Japan; it is in the Southeast, and it is the type of facility we need more of in the United States.

To compete beyond the 1980s, we need an emphasis on profits to support the investment necessary to compete effectively. It would help, of course, if the federal deficit could be reduced to free up more savings for investment. There will be major problems if the deficit is permitted to continue to absorb ever-greater resources from investment.

Many people turn to the government for help when competition becomes too great, when jobs are in jeopardy, or when communities are threatened by their companies' inability to survive under changed circumstances. It is not clear to me why we should turn to the government. How well has government demonstrated its ability to compete? How many jobs outside of the government itself has it really stimulated? How many communities have been given a new economic base through government action? This seemingly instinctive reaction is almost 180 degrees in the wrong direction. It is not government or even big business that creates economic growth. Establishments with fewer than 20 employees create jobs at a rate twice that of establishments with up to 1,000 employees. Actually, over the past decade, there has been a decline in jobs at the largest establishments, those with more than 1,000 employees.

The best and most sustainable growth comes from entrepreneurship. Another definition of profit might be "entrepreneurial return." Entrepreneurs are the ones creating jobs. They have an idea, a vision of a new, better, or different product that will make money, and they put that idea into action. If they fail, they will be back tomorrow with a better idea. Rarely do entrepreneurs manage large companies, though they may hire managers. They are risk takers, not risk avoiders. Like "profits," "entrepreneur" is a term with which we are not comfortable. Someone suggested to me that I refer to my husband as the CEO of an international miniconglomerate, since there is no term to describe what he does—except entrepreneur.

Few of the best of the high-performance companies in the Southeast would make the Fortune 500. Most are privately owned or closely held, essentially directed by the ideas of one or a few men. Generally passed over by the press, or their motives denigrated, these men are the true heroes of our age, men who just want to make money, to make a profit. They do not want something for nothing. They do not want to steal from anyone. They are not asking for a government handout. Generally they want to be left alone to deal with the marketplace and turn an idea into reality. Their profits, the golden fleece they seek, protect those around them, assure that our resources are allocated optimally, and provide investment and jobs for the future. What more could we ask of a hero? May they all find and keep the golden fleece.

KEN MILLEN

People Are the Key to Success

At MSA (Management Science America), I'm responsible for the people side of the business, in charge of recruiting, training, and developing our people. One of the things being discussed frequently is the shortage of people over the next few years. It's going to be an exciting time, and it certainly is going to be dependent upon finding and retaining qualified people.

We are a company that is focused on the technology side of industry. The silicon chip has changed our business in the last several years by making the computer available to more and more businesses.

Most people today are familiar with the computer, as well as the term "software." MSA is in the application software industry—the end products for which you use the computer. We are really into two aspects of application software: industry-specific software, the types used in manufacturing, banking, or insurance; and cross-industry software, things like general accounting packages and office productivity systems, which are used by all industries.

MSA was started by several young college graduates in Atlanta in 1963 as a consulting firm to the textile industry. It really started to grow in the late 1960s and into the first part of the 1970s. In the late 1960s, we grew from approximately 75 to 700 employees, and we were hiring 50, 60, or 70 people a week. We were setting up offices around the country.

One problem we were having during this rapid growth period was that our expenses were exceeding our revenues. There needs to be a focus on profitability, and we didn't have it at that point. We also lacked a business focus—we were trying to be all things to all people.

MSA filed bankruptcy, and John Imlay took over as our chief executive officer in 1971. He really looked at the company and saw that we were in several businesses. We hadn't decided what we wanted to be, what our focus was going to be, and we were doing a number of different things. We were a consulting operation, we were a service bureau, we had some software packages, and we also had the idea that anything that we attempted we probably should turn into a business. When we started sending people on airline trips, we decided to form a travel agency. When we bought a new office and started decorating it, we decided we should have an interior decorating subsidiary. We moved into unrelated fields.

John Imlay saw that major surgery was needed. He also saw that there was something of value in what we doing—that the software industry was going to experience rapid growth in the coming years. What he found of real value was a thing called the software package. He went through the process of taking the company from about 700 employees down to 50 in about one week. That was an interesting thing to do for someone who is known as being people-oriented.

Here's a true story. John Imlay was calling people out of various meetings to let them know he had to terminate their employment. At one meeting he called a gentleman out, brought him into his office and told him that, because of MSA's lack of profitability, he was going to have to let him go. The fellow became absolutely adamant and stood up and said, "There's no way you can fire me—I'm a customer." It turned out the man was a banker who had purchased our general ledger system. He was in a meeting to discuss installing the product.

Out of that whole process began the MSA of today. The company has grown from that point forward. MSA started over again in 1971 with approximately 50 people, as John Imlay began to formulate a purpose for the company. Companies need to decide what they are going to do and what each individual's commitment is going to be to corporate success.

Our first purpose was to build a profitable major corporation in the computer services industry with a personal touch. Before John Imlay, MSA was starting to build a major corporation, but it wasn't profitable. We decided to get the word profitable up front, and we decided we were going to be in the computer services industry. We were going to be a company in a high-technology field, but we were going to focus on the importance of people.

That started the theme setting of MSA. It's been a uniqueness that has contributed to our success. Each year at MSA we have a special theme. Frequently the theme is represented by an animal. It's a little risky having an animal doing this. One year we had a shark that was representing "Jaws" and our ability to attack the competition. All the shark did was sit in the bottom of the tank. You'll never see a slide of that shark.

What were some other themes? In 1979, we had Angel, the chimpanzee from "Fantasy Island." The theme that year was "Evolution or

Revolution"—what was really going to happen in our industry. Was it going to be an evolution or was it going to be a revolution, in terms of the company's growth and the direction of that growth?

The following year we featured a bear. The theme was the bull and the bear. It was the year we went public, and John Imlay wanted to emphasize to each of our employees the importance of going public— why we were doing it. The latest animal was a lion. We had two themes: "MSA, a Reflection of Me" and "Roaring into the 80s."

MSA has enjoyed revenue growth in excess of 40 percent per year. A subsidiary, Peachtree Software, is growing at a rate of 100 percent per year. What has this done in terms of people? MSA has grown from 70 employees in 1973 to 1,900 today. Certainly, the key to our success has been, and will continue to be, attracting the people to make our company successful.

We're located around the world. We have an opportunity in the software field to have a leadership position. We are now in a leadership role; to maintain that leadership is going to require lots of concentration on what we have to do to be increasingly productive in our ability to develop software.

We get a lot of visitors from around the world. The Japanese certainly are interested in the software industry. They have purchased a number of our systems. We are always a little concerned when they visit us because they ask astute questions. We can't decide whether they're really trying to learn about our software packages or whether they're trying to figure out how to start developing them. I'm sure they will be in that market in the foreseeable future.

MSA's whole theme has been that people are the key. At MSA that started with John Imlay presenting keys to the employees who came through the bankruptcy period with the company. Now we give a key from Tiffany's to each new employee and to their spouse. In our organization, the key is worn with a great deal of pride.

Here is a quote attributed to Andrew Carnegie that really hits the point: "Take away all my steel mills, take away all my money, leave me my people, and in five years I will have everything back." I'd like to focus on that.

The motto of the unmanaged employee is "I think I'm a mushroom: They keep me in the dark, they feed me cow manure, and when I grow up they'll can me." Well-managed employees need growth opportunities. Look at the software industry over the next several years—it will quadruple over the next five-year time frame. We translate that into opportunities to present to our employees.

We try to give our employees a focus on where we're going to be in some reasonable period. Right now we are looking at 1987, when we project an employee base of 5,000 people. The importance is not simply that we will have 5,000 employees. The importance is the opportunities that this can create for each one of our people.

We started five years ago with a career development program that is now our fundamental way of gaining and developing new employees. We've hired approximately 207 graduates over the last five years from colleges around the country. Approximately 181 of them are now working in our development organization, and 26 are in our field operations.

I have never seen college graduates more ready to work hard and to be successful. I've been recruiting people off college campuses for about 15 years, and I would say that in the last two to four years, the products the campuses are turning out are better than ever before. Today's graduates are ready to come to work. They're ready to succeed. It's up to us to provide the kind of environment to make that happen.

Abut 56 percent of our college graduates are computer science majors, with an overall grade point average of 3.1. The average age of an MSA employee is 31. It's a young group, a group that wants opportunities for growth.

Another aspect of a well-managed employee is one who is setting both personal and professional goals and who works for a company that allows them to happen. One of the things that makes MSA unique is that we have a limited amount of structure in our organization. When new people join our company we don't sit down with a sheet of paper that says, "In the first year, you will do these things and be promoted to this; in five years, you will do these things and be promoted to this." We don't have that kind of a structure. We're fighting hard to avoid it.

As we set our goals on being a billion-dollar software company, we intend to offer an opportunity for people to achieve their goals. If you analyze what people do, and how you keep productive people, you find that it's not so much the size of their paycheck as it is the challenges they are offered.

We place a premium on continuing to develop our people. We conduct management courses each month. These managers rate MSA on how well we're doing. They sit down with our chairman and president and establish effective two-way communication.

Grass-roots motivation is another characteristic of a well-managed employee.

We're famous for our themes, as I mentioned. In 1982, our kick-off program featured a cat theme. We took the Broadway musical *Cats* and rewrote the music to give it an MSA orientation. It wasn't done by any outside source; it was done by our own employees.

What are the key elements of motivation? How do you generate highly motivated, productive people? Where does it all start? It begins with a sense of purpose. MSA's purpose is to be the leader in information technology; we want to do it through innovation, quality, and customer service, and we want to continue to maintain a personal touch.

Each of our employees is familiar with this theme. They understand what we're trying to accomplish and how we're going to do it.

We are interested in long-range planning at MSA. We spend a lot of time on planning. But we also spend a lot of time communicating it to our employees. Each of our employees now has a goal fixed in his or her mind. It used to be a half-billion-dollar software company. Now our sights are set on being a billion-dollar software company. We're building it together, that's what is important. We make sure every employee knows the long-term goals.

Much of what we do is technology-driven. We try to maintain a state-of-the-art environment for our people. We've invested a lot in providing it.

We have fun together, as a company. We have our own softball program. It's not the competitive kind of softball program. We try to get everybody involved. If you want to have motivated employees, you need to keep them informed. It's impossible to overinform. The more you keep employees informed, the more motivated they are.

We have a monthly newsletter that goes to every employee in our organization. We've been publishing it for over five years. It's simple, but it gets a lot of information out quickly. When we set our goals, we try to put them in front of people. We have a new-employee orientation program. Our president, Bill Graves, attends these programs and has dinner with the new employees. It makes a big difference in terms of how people feel about their company.

Because people's impressions of an organization are based on their experiences during the first few days, we place a tremendous premium on getting our new employees together with the top management of the company. It was hard to do with 400 people, and it's harder with 2,000, but we're still trying to keep that personal touch.

People stay motivated in an organization that maintains a personal touch. Every employee recognizes the importance of this. At MSA, people are and will remain the key to our success.

MARVIN RUNYON

The Americanization of
Japanese Management

Our new venture in Tennessee is a result of a strong commitment that
Nissan Motor Co. Ltd. has made in the past two decades to increase its
leadership position in the international marketplace. Nissan began overseas production in 1966 with a manufacturing facility in Mexico. Today,
almost 20 years later, Nissan vehicles are produced in 20 countries around
the world.

Nissan Motor Manufacturing Corporation U.S.A. is the largest investment ever made outside of Japan by Nissan. In fact, with capital and
start-up expenditures of almost $660 million, it is the largest industrial
investment made by any Japanese company outside of Japan.

Nissan Motor Manufacturing Corporation U.S.A. was incorporated
in Delaware in July 1980, and we broke ground for our 3.4 million square
foot facility in February 1981. We built our first trucks for the United
States market in June 1983—two months ahead of schedule. We're currently employing over 1,800 people who are building over 8,000 trucks
a month.

We're in a unique position with our new company, because we have
been building a manufacturing facility and a company organization all
at the same time. We also have had the advantage of looking at the best
features of the American auto industry and combining them with the
best techniques and technology from Japan and other parts of the world.

Our Nissan engineers, contractors, and consultants have had to deal
with a number of challenging factors. First, our facility is large and
complex. For example, we have 78 acres under roof and utilize 229 robots
in the manufacturing processes. Second, we built on a greenfield site—
a cow pasture in rural Tennessee.

Third, we were on a fast-track schedule. Starting with a blank sheet
of paper, we completed the construction and equipment installation in
less than 28 months. We began construction without finished architectural and engineering drawings, and we started making equipment de-

cisions before the building designs were completed. We had to make decisions in half the normal time, and this required extremely close communication and cooperation—not only internally, but also with our suppliers.

As plans for the facility were being developed, our management team went around the world looking at other auto plants and talking with designers and engineers in order to find the latest state-of-the-art equipment.

The equipment in the Body, Frame, and Stamping Plant is mostly Japanese—built by Nissan—while the equipment in the Trim and Chassis Plant is primarily American. The Paint Plant adds an international flavor, with technologies from Germany, Sweden, Norway, Japan, and the United States, with all the equipment being manufactured here.

I'd like to give you some of the highlights of our application of technology in the manufacturing process.

- Our Body, Frame, and Stamping Plant is the most automated of our three plants. In Body Assembly we utilize 122 robots for spot-welding. The body assembly process requires 1,500 spot welds, and, as a result of the robots and hard automation, only 3 percent of the base vehicle requirements are done manually. We also have 54 welding robots that accomplish most of the arc-welding operations on the frame. We recently added four sealing robots that apply body sealer automatically.

- In our Paint Plant, state-of-the-art technology is employed in every phase of the painting operation.

  We currently utilize 36 spray robots and eight anticorrosion spraying robots in the paint process. We also have a Behr rotary atomizer, another type of automatic paint application that has laser beam controls to assure uniform distance for application to hood, roof, and bed of the trucks.

  All of the paint processes are monitored by the most sophisticated paint control system we know of. In the Paint Control Room, computers monitor over 3,000 checkpoints on oven temperatures, robot hydraulic pressures, humidity levels, and specific paint temperatures.

- In our Trim and Chassis Plant, we have two robots designed and build by our Smyrna employees for material-handling jobs in the tire assembly area. Last month we installed four additional robots in this plant to spray a rust-resistant finish onto the underside of completed trucks.

- We have a system for energy management, control, and monitoring of manufacturing processes and maintenance. It is probably the most state-of-the-art operation in our facility. This computer control system works through a network of fiber-optic cable transmitting signals throughout the plants, to connecting computers, programmable controllers, and other electronic equipment. It was designed specifically for Nissan by an Oak Ridge firm when existing technology proved to be inadequate for our needs.

- We're also using this system for transmitting a comprehensive video communications program to our employees. We have a television studio and control room in our administration building for producing and broadcasting live or taped television programs to over 100 monitors in meeting areas and other locations in the plants and the administration building.

  We're working on ways to utilize this capability fully. For example, we use the system, on a daily basis, for employee meetings, for training, and for general information purposes.

  We're the first automotive manufacturer to experiment with video communications to all employees. I don't know of another manufacturing operation that has as extensive an application.

All of this technology requires employees with skills different from those required by traditional industry. We need people with multi-skills to operate and maintain this sophisticated equipment. They must be able to solve problems and to work with other people in a team concept.

We think we have put together an outstanding group of employees, and we attribute our success to three factors. First, we had an opportunity to get to know potential employees and to see them in action during preemployment training. Second, we did extensive interviewing before employment. Finally, we were able to choose from an applicant pool of over 130,000 people.

Our hiring process for technicians has been unique. When we decided to build our plant in Tennessee, the state committed $7.3 million to preemployment training to help Tennessee residents acquire the basic skills needed to work in the automotive industry. For our part, we agreed to ease the state's unemployment problem by hiring as many Tennesseans as possible for our positions.

The first step toward a job at Nissan was for an applicant to be interviewed and accepted for preemployment training. State of Tennessee personnel did this screening, and we told them we were looking for people who were highly skilled in one area and were good candidates for cross-training in other skills. We also looked for people who were capable of a high level of cooperation and teamwork.

Preemployment training was conducted evenings or on weekends and continued at least six weeks. After people completed preemployment training, they became candidates for jobs at Nissan. Panels of three or four Nissan employees interviewed individual candidates, sometimes more than once. First-line supervisors participated in the interviews and always had a voice in who was hired in their areas.

In filling management positions, we looked for people who had strong technical skills, who were known to be good at their jobs—often with experience in the auto industry—and who were good and open with people. We also wanted people who were flexible, who would be open to new ideas. It all worked. I think we have an outstanding team.

From a management point of view, our new Nissan organization is unique. Our parent company in Japan maintained from the outset that we should be an American company with American management and employees. It has given us the flexibility to manage our employees the way we wish, as long as we maintain Nissan's high quality and productivity standards.

Most start-up situations have a degree of innovation, but many things are already decided. For instance, the corporate organization is in place, and the personnel policies, accounting policies, financial plans, and a large nucleus of management are already decided.

In our situation, we brought together two nationalities with very different cultures that had to work closely together. We also had several subcultures within the organization—those who had previous experience in the auto industry and those who did not, some who had third-party representation and some who had not—and we had no personnel policies, or any other policies, to transfer from an American parent company. So we had to create our own history as we began to evolve our management style.

How do you implement a management system like this? If the president of a company says this is the way he or she will conduct business, the decisions are imposed on people, and the results may or may not be effective. In our situation, we decided to gain input from all levels of the company by establishing goals all could agree upon. This would help create a value system that would be a common bond among all the employees.

We began with an initial survey, asking for input. We then conducted workshops with all employees in small groups, explaining how participative management could work and getting their ideas. Our employees gave us many ideas. Some brought back ideas from Japan. After many months, we came up with a corporate philosophy statement that unifies our employees and reflects their concerns. Many asked us why we were so slow in this process, but every suggestion was carefully considered and refined. We were able to avoid arriving at a decision too quickly and to avoid a "quick fix" that would not take into account many company and employee concerns.

Our philosophy states that our only objective is to produce the highest quality trucks sold in North America. In that document, we've outlined the components in meeting this objective. For instance, we state that people are our most valued resource, that all aspects of our business should reflect the highest standards of dedication and ethics, and that we're committed to making an economic and social contribution to the community and society at large.

Many of the words in our statement emphasize movement, such as constantly striving, developing, and growing. We always want to be moving toward something better. Teamwork is stressed throughout the statement and throughout the company, along with group decision making. In our company, we feel one person's problem is everyone's problem and that solutions arrived at by the group will be more likely to work better than unilateral decisions.

This also meant we needed to explore ways to develop a highly participative management style. We wanted everyone to have some input into the decision-making process. Participative management requires that people understand how to manage participation and that individuals learn to contribute beyond the confines of their jobs. In a system like this, followership is as important as leadership. That's a tough lesson for all of us who came up from the autocratic school.

We also looked at what was happening to American workers as we began to evolve a system in this new company. As you know, the values of employees in America have dramatically changed across the country. They're expecting greater involvement in decision making within their jobs. We also studied the fact that people work better when they share the same values.

Therefore, we decided early on that we would have five levels of management, instead of the usual 10 or 12 in most U.S. manufacturing companies. This was to assure that information could flow freely and openly from bottom to top and across company divisions.

Having fewer levels of management emphasizes our "sameness" as employees of Nissan, rather than the "differences" between bosses and workers. I see all levels of employees working together and mixing freely within our company. For example, our corporate contributions committee has representation from every level of our company, including hourly technicians. These technicians have as much voice as I have in making a $25 or $25,000 contribution. This cross-representation is evident in most of our committees and activities.

We all eat together in the same cafeterias and park in the employee parking lots. Many of us regularly wear company apparel, which is voluntary and provided to everyone without charge.

When we dedicated our new facility in October, we had 1,700 employees and 1,000 VIP guests. We gave the employees an equal opportunity with the guests to have front row seats. We asked a young woman who is a technician in our Paint Plant to speak at the dedication ceremony on behalf of our employees. She did an outstanding job. Mr. Ishihara, the president of our parent company, our governor, and a number of other dignitaries also spoke. But we all agreed that she stole the show. In fact, the Republicans and Democrats on the platform were fighting over her afterward.

Our management style also reflects the high degree of technology we employ in the manufacturing process. This demands that our employees be trained extremely well in a variety of skills.

Launch training was a major thrust for us. We spent a lot of time and money on it—about $29 million for the training of technicians and $23 million for management personnel.

Because of preemployment training, we started launch training with technicians who had already received up to 360 hours of instruction in welding, machine shop, hydraulics, pneumatics, electrical, or electronics, depending on their anticipated job responsibilities.

For launch training, we sent 383 supervisory personnel and technicians to Nissan plants in Japan to get actual "hands-on" experience. Over 95 percent of our technicians are Tennessee residents, most of whom have had no prior experience in an automotive manufacturing plant. Few had ever been out of the country. Some of our Tennessee employees had never been out of the state or on an airplane, so their Japanese experience had a profound impact on them in more ways than one.

We coordinated their training carefully, checking on what they were learning there. When they returned home, we picked up where they had left off. On the average, our technicians spent six weeks in Japan, although maintenance technicians spent, in a number of visits, an average of 23 weeks. Supervisory personnel accumulated as much as 40 weeks of training there, learning technical or manufacturing skills.

Instead of narrowly defined jobs traditional in the U.S. auto industry, we have four classifications for tecnhicians. Within each broad classification is a number of skills to be learned. We encourage our technicians to learn as many as possible.

All technicians are responsible for the quality of the job they do and for the maintenance of their tools. They take pride in being their own inspectors and tell me they appreciate having responsibility for the total job.

There's variety in the work, and they like it. They see more of the total production picture and understand how they fit in. And, because they have a number of skills, the degree of flexibility in our company is greatly enhanced.

We've built a time allowance into our production schedule for on-the-job training so a highly skilled technician can teach a less experienced technician another job right in the plant. We also give our skilled technicians special training so they will be effective teachers.

We do a lot of training in communications skills. Supervisors and managers are trained in orienting new employees, identifying group concerns, handling conflict positively, and a number of other topics. We count on this exchange of ideas to solve problems and improve our technologies.

We think these extensive training efforts are already paying off. We've gotten some excellent reports on the quality of the trucks we've built and favorable comments from our dealers and buyers. And, of course, our two-month-early start-up is another reflection of the success of our training programs.

Our concern for employees is also reflected in outstanding wage and benefits programs. Our wages are comparable to the American auto industry.

An Investment Security Program (or savings plan) allows our personnel to save a portion of their salary tax-free to which Nissan adds a matching amount from 60 to 100 percent.

We're putting in place a number of recreational and "wellness" programs for our employees and their families. At every break and meal period you see ping-pong, basketball, and volleyball games in and immediately outside the plants. We have a recreational area with a ball field, running track, swimming pool, and picnic shelter, and we recently opened a fitness center with Nautilus exercise equipment, an indoor track, and a regular schedule of fitness activities under the supervision of a staff.

All of this points out that we're not paying lip service to our employees when we say they "are our most valued resource." This commitment permeates every decision we make and every activity we undertake.

Our management style continues to evolve. We're constantly assessing, evaluating, and improving ourselves. We now have two important committees established, the Corporate Management Committee, which works as a team to look at the company as a whole, and the Directors' Council, which helps with problem solving. For all our employees, we now have employee involvement groups structured in groups similar to quality control circles. These groups work on company concerns as well as relations between our company and the community.

These efforts have brought us an exceptional work force that we consider as highly skilled and trained as you can find in the United States. It's too early to tell how successful we will be with this new approach to a traditional industry. We do know our employees across the board are excited about making it work. Most say it's the most positive work environment they have ever worked in, and they hope to be at Nissan the rest of their working lives. Naturally, we hope this enthusiasm will continue; we think it will.

All of us at Nissan Motor Manufacturing Corporation U.S.A. are pleased with the accomplishments of the past three years and look forward to the challenges we face in the future. I know that all of us in the American automotive industry have learned some valuable lessons, and I'm confident we all are headed in the right direction.

Audience Member: What is Mr. Runyon's monthly personnel turnover?

Marvin Runyon: We don't have any turnover.

Audience Member: Mr. Runyon, what's the primary difference in your facility, from management perspectives, versus what Nissan does in Japan?

Runyon: I'm not qualified to answer that question, because I've never studied the management practices in Japan. I know there are some differences in employee benefits. For example, employees in Japan are paid on the basis of age, seniority with the company, and family responsibilities. Two technicians have identical jobs on either side of the vehicle. One is 25 years old, lives at home, and is not married. The other has three children and may have a mother, father, and father-in-law living at home. The 50-year-old employee might make 50 percent more than the 25-year-old.

In the United States, of course, we don't do that because we pay equally for equal work. There can't be any kind of discrimination.

Another area is in the promotional aspects. In Japan, in the larger companies, there are no fast-track promotion policies like we have in the United States. You've got to work for a company for maybe 14 years before you can become a manager. In the United States, you could work in a company for two years and become a manager.

The Japanese system makes those people cooperate better and work better. If they've got a boss who's not so smart, they make sure that boss is successful. So, there are all kinds of ways that are beneficial. They don't have headhunters over there taking somebody from a competitor. You don't go from Nissan to Toyota and get a good job. You start over again if you change companies.

We haven't tried to take the Japanese way of managing and bring it in here.

Audience Member: I wonder if Mr. Runyon would comment on his company's position with regard to unions.

Runyon: We have no position. Third-party representation is determined completely by the employees. If they want a third-party representation, that's up to them. We think it works well to deal directly with our employees. We have only one objective in our company and that's to produce the highest quality trucks sold in North America. We think we can do that best by dealing individually with our employees and having them deal individually with us. The communications are much better and much faster, and problems can be solved immediately. We think it works well the way it is, and the employees, apparently, think so, too.

C. MARTIN WOOD III

Optimizing the Decentralized Approach

For as long as human beings have been around, there is evidence that they took fire, water, and some kind of either wheat or other grain, ground it together, and came up with something to eat. So baking has been around for a tremendously long time. It is truly what one might call a prosaic, ancient industry.

But at Flowers Industries, starting out in a part of the country where some still believe that a seven-course meal is an opossum and a six-pack of beer, we thought there might be a better way of doing things.

Flowers Industries is a Fortune 500 specialty branded foods company listed on the New York Stock Exchange. Our 1984 annualized sales will be around $600 million.

We have three operating divisions. First, we have our baked foods division, which specializes in traditional white bread, variety bread, hamburger buns, and rolls; I will concentrate on that operation a great deal. We have a snack foods division, which makes sweet snacks, cinnamon buns, chocolate roll cakes, cupcakes, Danish pastries, and most recently, cookies.

Finally, we have a convenience foods division, which concentrates on a very profitable niche of the large and prosaic vegetable industry. We concentrate on southern vegetables, such as okra, black-eyed peas, and yellow crook-necked squash. Coming from Connecticut, I didn't even know what an okra was; I thought it had four legs and a tail. But we have been successful in this industry. I'll point out that our convenience foods division, in a prosaic type of industry, generated a 14 percent operating income last year. When you put that in a context of what the overall vegetable industry has done in the past, you can see that it's been extremely profitable.

We are the only major baking company that hasn't changed hands in the past 26 years. In many instances, that change is still going on in the industry, because a lot of major baking companies that have changed hands once are doing it again.

Flowers Industries is decentralized. We operate 31 production facilities in 13 states. We run a distribution system that utilizes 300 tractor-trailer rigs and almost 3,000 route delivery trucks, so we are definitely in the trucking business. We employ about 10,000 people, with only 87 of those, from the janitor to the chairman of the board, located at corporate headquarters. Therefore, I think you would agree that we are decentralized.

We have produced consistent, dependable, predictable earnings growth of 16 percent compounded annually over the 15 years that we've been a publicly owned company. Our dividends have compounded at a 24 percent annual rate over the past 10 years—or, really, since our inception—and the past seven years have been characterized by four 3-for-2 stock splits.

But, above the financials, above the decentralization, we have a people orientation that has allowed us to do all of this. We truly believe that our people—and I'll put this in quotes, "The Flowers Family of Employees"—are our most important asset.

Now, why has Flowers been able to achieve superior results in an industry where others have failed? How have we succeeded when many others are failing right now in an industry that is characterized by overcapacity, by low margins, and by companies exiting the business rather than getting into it?

Why have we been successful, in many instances, using the same buildings, the same people, and the same equipment that our predecessors used? We think that it has to do with corporate philosophy: First and foremost, we believe that we are in business to make money for our shareholders; baking just happens to be one of the ways that we go about doing it.

We believe in high productivity that is achieved through attention to our employees, by making them part of the overall team. We believe in a lean management structure that has no brook with small bureaucracies and that keeps memorandums and other written communications to a bare minimum. We emphasize an action orientation that provides flexibility so we can adjust swiftly to changing times, changing market conditions, acquisition opportunities, and other corporate opportunities as they present themselves.

What's more, we believe that the spirit of entrepreneurship is fostered by maintaining operational autonomy, with decision making placed at the action level. The employees in the trenches, the ones actually doing the fighting, are the ones making the decisions for us on the front lines.

And, finally, we believe that the use of automation, combined with the reciprocal baking concept that we pioneered, allows us a competitive advantage as a least-cost producer in a highly competitive environment.

I'd like to address, individually, each one of those five major philo-sophical points. First, Flowers is in business to make money for its share-holders. Every company has this basic goal. Yet somewhere along the line it's possible to become so enamored of your product, or product line, or a potential acquisition, or your executive perquisites, or your corporate headquarters that you tend to lose sight of the original goal. You forget that, before the swamp became filled with alligators, your goal was to drain the swamp—or to make money for your shareholders.

Now, we have stated our goals publicly. We expect to be able to compound our earnings per share at 15 percent annually, indefinitely into the future. We expect to return 20 percent on shareholders' equity into the future, on an indefinite basis. Finally, we expect to return 15 percent on invested capital, after taxes.

These are not just targets we cooked up recently. They were stated publicly in 1972, when we were a much smaller company. We've achieved all but the last one. It's sometimes quite difficult to achieve an after-tax return of 15 percent on your invested capital when you make a career of buying busted bakeries and turning them around, putting the capital in place before any profits come onstream. We fully expect to be able to do that in the future, however.

We have grown by acquisition. We've grown by acquiring unprofitable operations, and we've grown by buying profitable operations. But we don't make acquisitions just because they're available. They must fit the overall corporate strategy to achieve our goals over a long and continuous period. We feel strongly that our shareholders prefer to invest in a com-pany that produces consistent, dependable, predictable earnings and div-idend growth over a protracted period of time, and that they are willing to pay a premium for the shares of a company that can achieve such a record.

Now, let's address the second philosophical point, that we achieve high productivity through attention to our employees by making them a part of the team. A great deal of emphasis is placed on imbuing our employees with the belief that their best job security, and their best potential for advancement, is achieved by helping to make Flowers In-dustries more profitable. This is extremely important when you're dealing with a company as decentralized as we are, where everybody has to keep an eye on the ball at the same time.

This emphasis on shared goals and values, with two-way channels of open communication, produces employees whose personal goals become consonant with those of the corporation. Our employees genuinely be-lieve that they are part of the "Flowers Family," a long-term corporate asset that, while not carried on the balance sheet, can significantly leverage the returns available on the company's hard assets.

Now, this is getting right at the heart of employee relations at Flowers Industries. We want everyone in our company to believe that they play a major part in the corporate role that management has set out: to be the most profitable company in the food industry. We want them to feel that they are personally responsible for part of our profitability. We seek to accomplish this through a variety of employee education programs. This is the crux of the matter when we start talking about decentralization.

We believe in a lean management structure, one that is flexible and capable of moving swiftly to meet a competitive challenge or to make an acquisition. There are no bureaucracies, there are few memos, and there is a tremendous action orientation at our corporate headquarters. There is tremendous goal orientation, with incentives based on goal achievement and performance, rather than on seniority or status.

I'm the senior vice president and chief financial officer of the corporation. Still it is quite possible that an employee's salary, bonus, and incentive bonus at one of our divisions could come to a good bit more than mine, based on the achievement of that division's goals. The corporation might not have achieved a goal that would allow me to participate. Therefore, it's quite possible that a division president, or a vice president, or even a plant president, could earn more in the incentive system than someone considerably senior to him in the corporate structure.

We believe in team cohesiveness. Our senior management team—the chief executive officer and six other officers—has worked together for a minimum of 12 years without anyone leaving and has an average age of 43 years. That has created what we consider to be a young, aggressive team of battle-hardened veterans that helped build the company from the $25 million in sales it posted in 1970 to the $600 million it should achieve this year.

We encourage dissent, and we encourage diversity of opinion until the quarterback calls the play. Then everybody pulls together to accomplish the mission as it's set out. Our senior management operates with the philosophy that there is absolutely no limit to where the company can go as long as no one cares who gets credit for a good idea. It's something we truly believe in and attempt to imbue in all levels of management.

Now, let's move to decentralization. We believe in fostering operational entrepreneurship. We use a centralized strategic planning function and decentralized operations. Each of our 31 producing operations is a profit center. Our product life cycle can be as short as 36 hours, from raw material to purchase in a grocery store. We must be able to respond to changes quickly.

Each market in the bakery business is different and has its own demographic, geographic, and competitive makeup. Atlanta is entirely different from Houston, Chattanooga, Miami, Jacksonville, or Tampa.

Each market has its own characteristics, so the plant president running the local operation must be able to take full responsibility for what we call the five "Ps." Those are the president's people, plant and equipment, the product mix sold in that market, the pricing, and the profitability of that plant, including the return on invested capital and return on assets employed in the business that we give the local executive.

Now, I want to step back just a minute, because I said that we believe in centralized philosophy and decentralized operations. Each plant, as far as its production goes, has its mission in life defined for it at corporate headquarters. Our plant president can't change that. Yet our short product life cycle dictates great emphasis on nimble, quick, effective management and a reporting system that allows the plant president to make accurate, timely, and prudent decisions.

We think we have the most sophisticated reporting system in the baking industry today. Each plant has its own data processing center—the computer, though not the programmers—to produce the operational reports needed to run that facility most effectively on a daily, weekly, and periodic basis. By Monday afternoon, all of the receivables for the previous week have been billed. By Tuesday morning, the plant president has a complete profit and loss statement on every single one of his production lines. By Tuesday afternoon, corporate headquarters has a consolidated weekly profit and loss statement, by plant and by production line, for all 31 operating facilities. Timely, accurate reports are absolutely essential to controlling the decentralized type of operation under which we operate. We must have them. Otherwise, we are so far away from the realities of the marketplace that we would be making decisions based on information we received two weeks earlier—information no longer even pertinent to the marketplace. This is a key to optimizing a decentralized operation.

I mentioned the reciprocal baking concept. It's part of our centralized strategic planning and our decentralized operation mode. Each plant's mission is defined at corporate headquarters. Is it going to be run as a bun and roll operation? Is it going to be a white bread operation, is it going to be a variety bread operation, or is it going to be some combination of those? In the case of a snack food division, are we going to bake sweet rolls in Crossville and snack cake in Spartanburg?

The baking business traditionally did all things in one place, under one roof. That was quite inefficient. You can imagine the number of changeovers that would be involved in baking in one Atlanta oven all the products that our Atlanta facility needed to serve its local market. It can't be done efficiently. Instead, our Atlanta plant is set up to run 16,000 pounds of white bread per hour with five people on the line. They handle it all, from the makeup room where the raw flour comes in, all the way through the wrapping machine.

Such automation allows us to virtually fix our in-plant labor costs and allows us to become the least-cost producer in the markets we serve. This is one of our operational goals, because we can take advantage of the competitive edge that this gives us in each individual market.

Now, the reciprocal baking concept functions around clusters of plants, for no one plant is an island. They are all interlocked by our over-the-road tractor-trailer system. Atlanta will bake white bread, not only for its own market, but also for our Chattanooga, Tennessee, facility and for all of northern Alabama—for facilities in Gadsden, Birmingham, and Opelika. It will then back-haul hamburger buns and hot dog rolls out of Birmingham and variety breads out of Gadsden, in full trailer-load quantities. They exchange products to serve the Atlanta market. That allows us to set up efficient, high-speed production lines that can run virtually around the clock.

What about the future of this decentralized operation? What about the future of Flowers Industries utilizing these concepts that are relatively new to our industry? We are stronger operationally and financially than we have ever been. We see more opportunities for continued growth, both internally and externally, through acquisition, than ever before. Our greatest strength lies in our southern geographic area, which is expected to grow substantially over the next 15 years. According to a recent article in the *Wall Street Journal*, 60 percent of all Americans will be living in the South and the West by the year 2000.

The South is our market area. This is where our great strength is, where we expect to be able to continue to improve on an internal basis. The West is the area that we are looking to for further expansion as we continue to grow via acquisition.

Finally, we have happy, dedicated employees, all of them shareholders of the company either through stock options, performance share awards, employee stock purchase plans, or an employee stock ownership trust.

By becoming shareholders, and thus owners in the company, all employees share the same goals as our top management team. To repeat, the major goal is to make money for our shareholders on a consistent, dependable, predictable basis. If we achieve this goal, then shareholders, management, and hourly employees will all be beneficiaries of our future success.

JOEL R. WELLS, JR.

Customer and Employee Feedback

I joined Sun Banks in 1975, having spent most of my career as a corporate lawyer in Orlando. While I had been a director of Sun Banks since 1967, my primary exposure to the bank was from a customer's point of view.

Sun Banks in 1975 was still a small company, comprised of a large Orlando bank and relatively small community banks. The banks were very people-sensitive, and they were quite aware of the communities they served. This attitude is probably best described by the founder of Sun Banks, Linton Allen, who said, "Build your community, and you build your bank."

Linton Allen was the first president of the First National Bank at Orlando, which opened in 1934. Another bank was already established in the market at that time. Today, Sun Banks holds 40 percent of the Orange Country market, whereas the other bank has less than 9 percent. What made the difference? We think Sun Banks' determination to build its communities set it apart from the other banks. No one called this philosophy "corporate culture" back then; it was simply the way to do business, an instinctive feeling.

About a year and a half ago, we reexamined our history. It seemed to us that we, like so many other expanding banks, had been moving away from our customers rather than staying close to them. Part of this was caused by the move to technology that was supposed to solve our back-office problems and make us more efficient. While doing this, we tended to forget some of our basic instincts in serving our customers, believing that technology would be the final answer. We were also growing substantially, and we realized that getting bigger did not necessarily mean getting better.

We formalized our strategy in 1982 with an announcement of our mission statement, which became the cornerstone of our new five-year strategic plan. Let me cite that statement: "The mission of Sun Banks is to promote the economic development and well-being of the communities served by the company, by providing citizens and enterprises with quality banking services in ways and scope consistent with high professional and ethical standards, a fair and adequate return to the company's shareholders, and fair treatment for the company's employees."

Our strategy became one of pleasing our employees, who in turn react more positively to customers. A pleased customer, then, should result in more business to the bank and higher stock prices and dividends to shareholders.

To find out how good—or how bad—a job we were doing, we developed an employee attitude survey and a customer attitude survey. All of our employees took the survey. We mailed out the survey to almost 10,000 customers and received a 44 percent response—pretty overwhelming.

Our employees responded that they like the people they work with, they like working with customers and pleasing them, and they like the company; 87 percent said they are proud to be a Sun Banker. On the minus side, employees said that pleasing the employee is not a high priority in the company and that employee training and career counseling programs are underdeveloped.

We felt that we had, overall, satisfied employees, but we wanted to turn them into pleased employees. Our response to employees was to seek better hiring, better training, better policies, more management involvement, and more employee involvement.

Specifically, we founded Sun Bank University, where all employees can receive consistently high-quality training. We began a Branch Managers' Academy to develop more highly skilled managers. This is an outgrowth of our new Branch Managers Council, which meets monthly. We also created a Sun Bank Video Network, a monthly program of key events within Sun Banks. It is a 15 to 20 minute video tape presentation shown to all employees. And we launched what we call the Sunsuggestion Program, which generated over 2,000 suggestions and earned almost $30,000 in awards for 300 people.

To get management more involved, we introduced a work-sharing program where the top holding company and bank executives spend one day every other month helping customer-contact people. This means serving as a teller, making consumer loans, handling customer inquiries at the computer center, and working with credit card customers. Not only do those of us at the executive level get to see how the customers are being treated, but we gain a better understanding of job conditions for our customer-contact employees.

In addition, we started a program of management-by-walking-about. This idea came directly from the book *In Search of Excellence*. I took it to heart and visited each of our 175 Sun Bank branch offices and all of the employees this past year. That is the best time I have ever spent with the company. Meeting the employees, listening to them, and seeing their working environment was a tremendous experience for me personally.

Our most recent effort to please employees is our proposed new Sun-share program, which shareholders will consider at our upcoming annual meeting. This plan would allow for a 100 percent matching contribution by the company on up to 6 percent of an employee's salary, with all funds to be invested in Sun Banks' common stock.

Sunshare is tied into a 401K deferred compensation plan, so the employee's contribution would not be taxable income at the time of contribution, only when he or she withdraws it. We expect that all our eligible employees will join this plan, making them significant shareholders over time.

We have set specific, measurable goals to track our progress in pleasing employees. Our timetable is to attain these goals annually to reach a five-year target. The first goal is to reduce employee dissatisfaction by 10 percent per year. Second, we want to reduce the number of non-entry level positions filled from the outside by 15 percent per year, emphasizing a promote-from-within policy. Finally, we hope to reduce employee turnover by 15 percent a year.

This program was begun in the second quarter of 1983, and we have done rather well so far. The top "pleased employee" score, measured through the employee survey, is 4.0. We achieved a 2.99 score in our first survey. I'd call that a solid B average. We're shooting for at least an A −.

Our next goal—reducing the percentage of jobs filled externally—is a tough one. It means stronger management training programs, and it means giving our own people a better shot at higher positions.

The third goal—reducing employee turnover—is progressing quite well: turnover averaged about 28 percent in 1983, and we are attempting to bring it down to 18 percent by 1987. The 18 percent turnover rate that we use as a goal is the one the Disney organization already has attained in the Orlando market. Disney has similar customer-oriented employees.

Pleasing customers is extremely difficult—a bigger challenge, by the way, than pleasing your employees. We had to find out what was on their minds. So we sent out a long questionnaire, and we received a great 44 percent response. Judging from that response we knew the survey was a good idea.

We didn't make any great discoveries, but we generally confirmed our beliefs about what customers wanted: courteous, efficient service and error-free service. The largest performance gaps cited by customers were weaknesses in clear, understandable monthly account statements, in our accuracy in handling accounts, and in simple loan approval procedures. We also found a great opportunity to cross-sell our customers, since we discovered that our customers were buying from other financial institutions more than half of the services we were selling. What an opportunity for us! I've heard the phrase "new business" as though new customers provide all the growth. Well, we're interested in more business, and existing customers are the best source.

Since we completed that survey, we have installed some measurement standards for pleasing our customers. We set one goal of reducing avoidable account closings by 10 percent per year, and another goal of increasing average usage of core services by 10 percent per year.

What are the results to date? We are presently selling 2.55 services to each customer. That is well above the national average, but our goal is 3.8. We have our work cut out for us in reducing avoidable account closings to reach our goal of 27 percent by 1987.

We are also trying to communicate more often with our customers. One idea we came up with was to send them a periodic message with their monthly statements. We call it "Sunbeams." We have received many letters from our customers saying, in effect, "Thank you for asking us what we think."

Our strategy to please employees and customers should result in pleasing our shareholders. We have set four goals for ourselves in this area. Three of them are achieving a return on earning assets of 1.1 percent, achieving a return on equity of 15 percent, and achieving an internal capital generation rate of 10 percent. In 1983, we attained one of those three goals: exceeding our targeted 15 percent return on equity.

Our fourth goal is to exceed the earnings per share growth of at least half of our peer group in two out of three years. We accomplished this in 1983, and my incentive compensation is tied to it, so I consider it pretty important.

What about the price performance of our stock? We are proud of the fact that for eight consecutive years our stock price has been higher at the end of the year than it was as of the previous year-end. But we want to see that trend continue and perhaps even grow on an annual percentage basis.

At Sun Banks, then, we have made a commitment to our people and our customers, and we believe we have the system in place to make our commitment work.

Audience Member: Mr. Wells, how lengthy were the customer and employee surveys as far as numbers of questions?

Joel Wells: They were lengthy and detailed. They were not cursory questionnaires at all. Because of that, we were particularly pleased with the responses.

GERALD EICKHOFF

Leveraging a Consulting Operation

Jim Cotton and I founded Bank Earnings International (BEI) in 1976, after we had worked for Citizens and Southern National Bank (C&S) in Atlanta, managing various phases of operations. At BEI, we utilize some of the expertise and management philosophies developed at C&S and transfer those to banks around the country. Early successes and the close client relationships that followed have allowed us to position ourselves in a changing marketplace. We now have about 125 employees with headquarters in Atlanta and regional offices in Dallas and San Diego.

BEI is still privately held, with an average return on equity for the last seven and a half years of 47 percent per year. We are highly leveraged and are fortunate that we have been able to generate all of our capital requirements internally.

There are several reasons for our growth and success. First, the changes in the deregulated financial industry have had a tremendous impact on our ability to grow. We have expanded to meet the challenges and opportunities of change.

Second, we've been able to attract and retain high-caliber, qualified people, and we've had virtually no turnover. From a base of over 120 employees, we've lost 13 people in seven and a half years. We offer opportunities for people, and that's why they stay.

Third, we initiated a pricing philosophy that helped distinguish us from other consulting firms. Because we employ only former bankers with management backgrounds and because of their experience in specific disciplines within the industry, we are willing to price our services based on a percentage of the actual first year's bottom-line improvement generated through the implementation of our programs. This contingency was unique in consulting, and the fact that we were being paid on measurable results was refreshing to the banker.

We also price on the typical time card, or flat fee, by multiplying our hourly rate times the number of hours required. However, most of our clients choose the percentage approach because they know they're going to get what they pay for. We have incentive and so do they.

Fourth, we demand client satisfaction. If a client is not satisfied at the end of an engagement, we either stay and make it right or take care of it in some other way. Our clients are our lifeblood. The industry is too small and the relationships too close for us not to insist on satisfaction and results. We've grown in large part through references from that client base and additional contracts from former clients. We've got to nurture our clients.

Fifth, we implemented a rigorous three-year planning process. We meet off-site every six months to update the plan. We drop off the previous six months and add the next six months, so we know where we're going, and target the size firm we want to be. We just finished the third year of the first plan, and we were just one employee off the projections we had made three years earlier and $100,000 over on the revenue side. We have been able, through working as a team and going off-site, to plan where we want to go. But the industry we serve has no such plan, and the last few years have been dramatic, challenging and filled with opportunity.

ENVIRONMENT OF THE FINANCIAL INDUSTRY

Merrill Lynch's introduction of its Cash Management Account (CMA) led the financial industry to talk about competing on a level playing field. The industry began lobbying Congress to deregulate both sides of the balance sheet. The resulting problems left for the financial industry have been traumatic.

Several larger commercial banks have gotten in trouble by seeking the highest possible return on their asset base. When a bank consistently puts its money out at the highest return, there will be problems. A lot of that money flowed overseas and may never return. That has created pressure on some of the big money center banks.

By deregulating both sides of the thrift industry, the savings and loans borrowed their money at 14, 15, and 16 percent, loaned it out at 9 percent, and tried to make up the difference on the margin in volume. That won't work in any industry. Now they've gotten a reprieve as rates have fallen off, but as rates pick back up, you'll see pressure coming back on that industry.

Additionally, a major demographic shift in the United States over the last 10 years is having a tremendous impact. We have less than 1 percent growth in the U.S. population base now. Over 90 percent of that growth is in the Sun Belt, primarily Florida. That means we don't have the influx of new customers into the marketplace that we had with the baby-boomers.

As inflation ebbs and as the growth rate of the money supply is reduced, more organizations are competing for fewer customers and fewer dollars. We currently have tremendous competition among the financial conglomerates, the giants in the commercial banking system, and the thrift industry.

When the *American Banker* newspaper surveyed the nation's top 2,000 bank CEOs, 93 percent said the major competitors concerning them today are their brother banks and thrifts. In 1990, however, they predict their number-one competitor will be Sears. The reason Sears is so powerful is that it already has a full financial supermarket operating. It has a credit card base of 40 million customers. It has a franchise on those customers and is serious about getting into the financial industry.

The CEOs targeted Merrill Lynch to be number two, Shearson/American Express number three, Prudential Bache number four, E. F. Hutton number five, Aetna number six, and Kroger number seven.

In the future, there can be only continued consolidation and blurring. There will be increased interstate and interregional bank acquisitions. More franchising programs will be introduced. Banking will look similar, in many respects, to the Century 21 and ERA real estate networks, to the Coca-Cola bottling network, or to Chevrolet dealerships—all of which are franchise operations. There will be an increased need for improved productivity and fee income generation in the banks. These are areas in which we specialize.

Right now the consultants and the sign makers are doing well. BEI's challenge is to stay in advance of all this change, both from a conceptual standpoint and a technological standpoint. We work hard at doing that. We're maintaining and continuing to hire high-caliber, qualified people. We've got to keep building our satisfied client base and seeking new opportunities.

BEI LEVERAGE

Our corporate philosophy is as follows: First, we hire only former bankers, mortgage bankers, or thrift managers. We take only experienced people. There have been few exceptions. This certainly shortens our training cycle, and when we put somebody in a bank or a savings and loan to consult, they have many years of experience in that area.

Second, we deliver our product and price based on quantifiable results. In other words, we take a fee based on 25 to 35 percent of the first year's annualized benefit, plus out-of-pocket expenses. We get paid based on what shows up on the bottom line.

We gear the compensation of our key people to incentives and strongly encourage the entrepreneurial spirit. Simply stated, we are a small group of entrepreneurs who run across opportunities and who make those opportunities available to the people in our organization able to handle them.

Customer service, with us, reigns supreme. To succeed, we must have satisfied clients. We are aware that it is easier to run a small company than it is to run a larger one. To be good after many years of operation is a tremendous testimony for companies such as Delta or Wachovia or Trust Company of Georgia.

The three ways we leveraged the firm are in the areas of employee productivity, pricing, and new ventures in our marketing techniques.

First, the working environment at BEI is loose. All our consultants have a four-day work week, which means three nights on the road, typically, and Friday in the office if they so choose. We don't demand extra duty, for we believe the job can be done in a reasonable amount of time. Most consulting firms keep their people on the road four nights and five days and work them a half day on Saturday. We think that's how you burn out people.

Second, in terms of cash remuneration, the compensation we give our people is composed of two things. The first is the base salary. If they come out of a financial institution, they will usually make 10 percent more in base salary with BEI than they were making. The second is an incentive compensation program geared to the profitability of the company and the individual's performance. We pay this bonus every six months. The result is that everybody feels so close to the next bonus that they can't afford to leave. It has worked to our advantage. Last year, those two bonuses averaged 64 percent per employee. The employees, therefore, maintain a great interest in our earnings.

EQUITY INCENTIVES

At BEI, we have minority equity participants in our subsidiaries. Our corporate structure includes BEI Holdings, the parent company, presently owned 100 percent by my partner and myself. There are five operating subsidiaries, each with a president, who has an equity position in that company. If we sell out or go public, their stock would be convertible at its value.

We're making 10 percent of our holding company's stock available to all employees, from the clerical ranks up to the top, based on seniority and position. We will be placing what we think is a valuable commodity in the hands of our people. Mills B. Lane, chairman of the C&S Bank several years ago, once said that he never found a better way to motivate people than by making them rich. We at BEI agree with this philosophy.

A major priority has been to maintain low turnover. If we had to keep training new people, we would lose momentum. The faster we complete projects, assuming we're on a percentage basis, the higher our yields.

Our staff has free usage of microcomputers. This use is encouraged. If individuals want to develop software that allows them to be more productive on their jobs and we can train other people to use it, they have carte blanche to do so.

People who get things done are not always the easiest to manage. We have chosen product quality over tranquil management. High-performance men and women with big egos and high-drive profiles, and who give special challenges in terms of managing, tend to gravitate to our firm. A large number of them have been fired previously. They are hard to structure but can fill vacuums. In an environment where you attract that kind of person, as we want to, you must give a lot of rope.

PRICING POLICY

Bank Earnings has developed yardsticks in banking that allow a CEO to see whether he's doing what is appropriate in certain areas. The typical CEO does not come out of an operational environment, but is a commercial lender without real hands-on, high-level experience in operations. Sometimes it's difficult to tell how good or how not-so-good things are.

The yardsticks determine appropriate productivity levels, how much fee income should be generated, and what float ratios should be. Those are the ratios we check off with the chief financial officers of organizations in advance of doing a project to ensure that what we implement shows up in that format.

The fees are mutually agreed upon in advance. They also are mutually agreed upon at the time of payment. If we say we will produce $1 million of benefit, and it tracks out at $1 million, we get paid on that. If it's $900,000, our fee is based on that figure. Our minimum man-week yield is $5,000. In a good situation, where the bank is moving forward and wants to get things done, we can improve those yields substantially.

BEI JOINT VENTURES

Recently, BEI has begun joint ventures with Fortune 500 companies to fill a need by utilizing our specific niche in the marketplace. The first one we put together was with EDS, Ross Pirot's data processing firm in Dallas. We helped EDS expand its sales to the financial industry.

BEI's joint venture with the *American Banker*, the largest daily newspaper in banking, is a research study on the future usage of microcomputers in the financial industry. The *American Banker* marketed it, and we're doing the research. We put a low price of $2,750 on it, and in a period of 60 days, sold over 210 memberships to fund the research.

The success of that program was noted by Dun & Bradstreet Corporation, whose annual sales last year totaled $1.7 billion. They presently have everything you want to know about six million U.S. corporations and 80 million American households in their database.

We're now involved in two joint venture studies with Dun & Bradstreet on usage of microcomputers in the corporate area. Dun & Bradstreet will do the marketing for us, and we'll do the research. The price again will be $2,750. Our targeted goal is to have 2,000 members. We're leveraging off somebody else's tremendous reputation and dollar ability to put a project together, yet we are filling an important niche.

The philosophy of these big companies is changing. They're not interested in trying to build everything today. They're also not interested in trying to acquire everything. Big companies have found they demotivate small companies when they buy them, because they can change the entrepreneurial flair. So, now they're joint venturing with smaller companies.

We also have entered into a joint venture with First Nationwide Financial Corporation of California, a $9 billion savings and loan that is the second franchiser in the financial industry business. We're franchising its name and all the BEI products. First Nationwide's network presently has nine members with $4.5 billion in assets and is profitable now.

The response to that program has been extremely positive. We know six more major commercial banks are developing franchise programs or are actively researching the concept. It's a way for smaller local organizations to maintain ownership and control without having to sell out.

We are dedicated to building BEI Holdings with its core sales force, and continue to do what we do best. At the same time, we want to leverage out with other major companies to take advantage of their expertise, add our expertise, and grow. We're now perceived as a joint venture candidate for companies smaller than we, and we're looking seriously at all these possibilities.

PRESTON MARTIN

Innovation, Productivity, and Economic Policy

A most appropriate matter to be addressed in the current controversy over economic growth and disinflation is the role of innovation and productivity. You are certainly familiar with the indications of a strong expansion in this country, reflected in the quarter-by-quarter numbers. Of course, the question in the minds of Federal Open Market Committee members and others is whether the expansion is coming too fast. Is the economy overheating, or do we simply have some overheated economists? That is a question I believe we must continually address; it is that important.

Part of the argument turns, of course, on whether some magic figure exists for utilization of capacity in manufacturing and whether we've approached a capacity limit. Is 80 percent the magic figure? Or is it 82 or 85? Is capacity too slippery a number now that we are importing, in some cases, 30 or 40 percent of our consumer goods as well as substantial volumes of producer goods, machine tools, even heavy machinery? Is the U.S. capacity figure as important as it used to be? You can tell from the way I'm approaching this subject that I don't think it is.

Capacity utilization is one of those measures of activity and of possible oncoming inflation of historic importance. But this may be a changed world economy. The United States is involved in global trade so deeply now that analysis cannot stop at domestic capacity utilization. Likewise it is insufficient to simply draw the pattern of the last five recoveries since World War II and say, "Here is where inflation began in each of these recoveries, and we are approaching that capacity utilization level again." It's not that simple. We may have a different resource allocation and a different outlook as far as economic growth and inflation are concerned this time.

So, perhaps we should concentrate further on the productivity side of the economy question. There are two schools of thought: The statisticians say that, though productivity went up 3.1 percent last year, the rise is only what the economy experienced in past postwar recoveries. The new orders come in, management hasn't had time to restaff, and of course you get more output per person, per hour. This school argues that is to be expected.

Then there are analysts such as John Kendrick, of George Washington University, studying this question. Kendrick argues that there have been fundamental changes in a number of forces and factors pointing to more than a cyclical recovery. We may be back into a pre-1970s configuration, say analysts like Kendrick; we're back into the sort of economy that prevailed in the 1950s and 1960s. If so, that might mean we should get back on a trend line of perhaps a 3 percent increase in output per person, per hour. In turn, this could mean that inflation would not come back as strongly as it did in recovery X, and Y, and Z.

The evidence is not conclusive on either side. The statistical evidence I cited is well known. You can graph the first year of this recovery against those other recoveries, and we are tracking right with previous comparable periods. The question is, where do we go from here? Is this, as some argue, a new kind of performance? Will production indirectly ameliorate some dilemmas that we face—the high federal mega-deficit, the very high current-account deficit, and the lofty interest rates? And what about the question of sustaining a recovery this time? Can we achieve a three-or even a four-year growth period before the next recession?

There is no question of our need for economic growth; we have an imperative to reinvest, both in the public and the private sector. Among other less-developed countries (LDCs), Brazil has been building automobile plants and steel mills. You could iterate this around the other LDCs. At a time when the United Kingdom has gotten hold of its productive facilities a bit, along with the Germans, the French, and others, we have been consuming our capital.

We need to restore our productive capacity in the private sector. We also need the roads, bridges, railroads, and all the rest of the public infrastructure that we've been using up. Do you remember the last time you were in New York, Philadelphia, or Boston? Do you remember the roads and how you could use a bridge one day and not the next? It isn't just an East Coast phenomenon—in our consumer economy that we all enjoy, we may have consumed the "seed corn."

How can we reverse this trend? Can we reinvest adequately in productive capacity, as we are beginning to do? Can we build back the infrastructure at the same time consumers are making up for all those obsolete cars they have driven the last several years? Can we reinvest at the same time that those people who have been living in apartments, and now have a child or two, are entering the housing market? Can we meet all these needs simultaneously, while the federal government runs those mega-deficits that boggle the mind? The necessary environment includes restoring a substantial rate of economic growth. You do it not by balancing down, but by expanding the economic thrust of the society.

The other side of that coin is potential inflation. If we are truly committed to a disinflationary policy, and if it is so vital, can we accelerate economic growth at the same time? Can we return to a trade trend-line rate of economic growth that allows us to rebuild, reinvest, and restore our world competitive position without reigniting inflation?

That may be the dilemma of all dilemmas. Can we accomplish that? Part of this apparently contradictory set of objectives lies behind the debate about an industrial policy—aping the indicative planning mode of the French government.

However, there may be some way to resolve these goals and objectives that apparently are in contradiction with each other. Part of the answer to achieving substantial growth, while pursuing a disinflationary set of policies on the monetary side, lies in restoring productivity. In a sense, that is what you're dealing with at this conference.

If a key factor in economic growth is productivity, then how does it look? From World War II until the 1970s, productivity grew on average about 2.5 percent annually. If you formed your opinions about the U.S. economy years back, you remember how startling it was to learn that there were recent years in which productivity fell. Indeed, productivity growth slowed to under 1 percent per year from 1980 to 1983.

However, in the last recession we began to see the numbers swing positive again. Then in the fourth quarter of 1983, the growth in productivity was virtually flat. This was in part a cyclical phenomenon, occurring because so much hiring took place that year. Augmentation of the labor force was substantial because, in many cases, these were people being recalled to jobs. The pessimists who said some of these people being laid off would never be reemployed, anywhere, were, once again, wrong. Many of the first people hired seemed to be the ones that had been laid off. Surely, there have been changes; many workers have been going back into a different job configuration, maybe a different plant, a different office, or a lower compensation. Just the same, we have been adding something like 300,000 to 400,000 people a month to the employed labor force since the rebound started. By one measure, we added four million employees to the goods and services production lines and offices of this country in the short space of the recovery to date.

What about the future? What can we expect of this labor force? Has the growth in productivity returned, and is the fight against inflation a manageable one? There is a growing school of thought that productivity is improving not so much because we are working smarter, but because some of the external constraints to the economy are not dragging down our growth. These analysts mention the two oil shocks and what they meant in terms of restructuring and productivity in the 1970s. They anticipate that this phenomenon won't repeat itself in the decade to come. Likewise, they look on the output from the food production sector as encouraging.

As for the rapid expansion of the labor force in the 1970s, these new entrants of the last decade now have some experience. The rehiring of so many people last year does not mean a wave of inexperienced hands. There has been a slowing in the rate at which women are entering the labor force and in the number of young workers taking jobs for the first time.

We've seen a slowdown in the wave of new regulations that business people have experienced. These came out of political action, and each addressed a valid social problem. Yet each resulted in businesses having to bear costs in dealing with emissions, safety, and so forth, rather than spending as much capital to improve productivity. Several students of the subject say there doesn't seem to be as much attention paid by Congress or the incumbent administration to those concerns.

We are all aware of the anecdotal evidence of productivity improvement, such as in the field of labor settlements. And we are seeing improvement not just in compensation, but in the flexibility and definition of the job and in changes in work rules.

During the remainder of this conference, you'll hear experts in the field comment on whether these changes—on the job, in the work rules, and in output-related compensation—are taking place. The question for economic policy is whether we will be able to encourage this trend across the board, not just in some of the spectacular success stories that President Forrestal and his colleagues have focused on during this program. Consider, as you hear these success stories, whether they represent only exemplars, or whether they can provide general guidance in our thinking about growth and disinflation—whether these practices, at least to some degree, can permeate the whole work force and the whole economy.

If these innovative techniques and approaches can be generalized across the whole labor force, I think we may conclude that productivity is going to be substantially different and that we have an opportunity to return to something like the old growth trends. If that proves true, inflation may be less of a problem in the decade to come.

A number of legal and institutional restraints on the economy have been changed. You know what the Economic Recovery Act of 1981 has accomplished in terms of depreciation, write-offs, and cash flow. Business spending—this fixed investment boomlet that's now upon us—should be no surprise, when you think of the cash-flow situation of U.S. industry and the impact of the tax changes.

The monetarists have to be right occasionally, the Keynesians on other occasions, and the supply-siders at still other periods. Maybe the supply-siders can teach us something about the productive potential in tax incentives, marginal tax rates, and cash flow. Certainly, the venture-capital flows have been restored since the 1978 capital-gain tax changes.

So, these are factors to consider. You and I know that attitudes don't really change. Institutions can be slow to adapt. Once the order book gets filled and management "stocks out" a few times in inventory, resistance weakens, allowing the union to define the job. There is a recurring cycle in human affairs. You can build a case that, once we recover to something approaching full utilization of resources, back we will go to the old ways.

Audience Member: Are Wall Street's fears really sound ones: Are we going into a period of high interest rates?

Preston Martin: We're already in a period of high interest rates. Are you asking which way the pressures look like they're going? In the short run, the pressures are toward higher interest rates, because we've had more of an upswing in first-quarter 1984 corporate financing needs than many Wall Streeters thought would occur so soon. We've all been aware of the huge cash flow in corporate America.

I've got a question in writing I'd better read.

"Real interest rates have remained positive at spreads that are historically high. Please comment on the factors causing this relatively new phenomenon, the degree of cause from deposit deregulation, on the cost side, versus federal deficit financing, on the demand side, and the likelihood of these large positive spreads continuing into the 1990s."

Bankers will tell you their costs of funds have gone up about 100 basis points, or 150, or even close to 200 basis points. Those costs are higher. But just because your costs go up does not necessarily give you the ability to raise prices. The costs represent a factor. Yet, we must have deregulation. It is fantastic to go on, decade after decade, with the federal government setting the interest rates paid savers on various kinds of instruments.

There isn't any magic formula, such as getting 100 basis points relief in interest rates for every $50 billion the deficit is reduced. It doesn't work that way. But rates are too high in a real sense.

In the long run, the real rate of interest trend line in this country may be 3 percent or 2.7 or 3.2. Add an expectation of, say, 5 percent inflation, and you still don't get today's interest rates. They're even higher than that.

All of us are holding our breath for action on fiscal bills by

Congress. Some tangible action to bring these absurd federal deficits down should give us some offset to all this demand.

Audience Member: What would be the best response to a demonstrable change in Congress's attitude on the deficit?

Martin: A huge sigh of relief would be our response. We, of course, are in a dilemma, and given the demand for funds, and given what the market is doing to interest rates, how do we discharge our role of sustaining the economic recovery? Your answer might be that we should stop the rise in interest rates in the short-term market by providing enough reserves. But then what will happen to interest expectations in the long market? We could, for some time, temporarily top off the short rates. But then you trigger the inflationary expectations of the traders who have gone over and over again to their boards of directors and said, "I'm sorry but we lost another $5 million because I again bought long bonds." Those people have become rather sensitive—those who are working at their old jobs.

Our response would be that it would give us more action space, as the mathematicians say, to conduct monetary policy—a broader field within which to work.

Audience Member: Can you explain the recent Fed decisions that supported interregional banking?

Martin: The questioner is alluding to Florida, where we let a bank come in from out of state to do banking business, and to Massachusetts and Connecticut, where we approved the acquisition of banks across state lines. In each of those cases we gave our approval, with the greatest of reluctance, based on the statute we have to administer. That statute and court decisions say to the Board of Governors, sit as though you were passing on the constitutionality of state law dealing in the banking area, such as a state law that permits a bank holding company from one state to buy a bank in another state. Our response has been that we're not a court, and the Congress or the Supreme Court should decide these matters. Our actions in those cases were taken with the greatest reluctance, and in decisions we told Congress: Set up the rules of the game. Don't force the Board of Governors to sit as a judicial body and pass on the constitutionality of state law.

JOHN A. SAVAGE

Growth and Success through Employee Motivation

William N. Cox, Moderator

One of the most interesting parts of our research into high-performance companies is that we have found, as authors Bob Waterman and Tom Peters found before us, that superior companies are doing similar things regardless of industry. Indeed, the whole concept of industry may be outmoded today, and I think you're seeing that come through in these presentations.

We're going to revisit one of those common themes, the theme of productivity through people, the theme that your best assets go out of your building every night in the elevators—that people are your most important asset.

Now, many decent-sized companies will have a mission statement that says something like, "productivity of our people is most important." The words are all similar, and I would even go so far as to say that most senior management people, when they read Waterman and Peters's book In Search of Excellence or when they read our research on high-performance organizations, probably will say to themselves, yes, sir, that's us.

Yet it's interesting to put that side by side with a recent survey by the Yankelovich organization, one of the most sophisticated polling groups in the United States.

That organization went to the American worker and asked a very simple question: Do you think that if you improve your productivity, and your personal contribution to your business, you will benefit, personally, from that productivity? This is the acid test. Fully seven-eighths of the workers polled said, no, I don't think it will benefit me if I improve my productivity and my contribution to this organization.

Something is haywire here. What it means is that although many companies have mission statements that say, in effect, "people are our most important asset," the turkeys obviously are saying the same thing as the eagles.

What the next four gentlemen have in common is not that they say people are our most important asset, but that they are demonstrating it. The success of their organizations and the testimony of their employees say that these executives, like the ones we heard from earlier, are indeed eagles and not turkeys.

A fascinating combination of companies is represented. We have a steel producer, a hospital management company, a supermarket operation, and one of the most distinguished banks in the Southeast. They represent quite a cross-section, but I think you will hear, as we have heard in our research, that the things they are doing are quite similar.

To begin with, I would like to introduce John Savage, manager of personnel services for Nucor Corporation in Charlotte, North Carolina. It's a company that is succeeding, just as we heard of Flowers Industries, in an industry where "it can't be done." What's more, Nucor is doing it without government assistance, and doing it, genuinely, with productivity through people.

The others in this diverse session are William Fickling, Jr., chairman of Charter Medical Corporation; Mark Hollis, a vice president of Publix Super Markets; and Robert Strickland, board chairman of Trust Company of Georgia.

While Nucor's incentive compensation programs have received considerable publicity, we cannot look at our productivity improvements solely in light of those programs. Instead, it is necessary to look at a number of factors that have had a great deal of significance in our success.

First is the basic philosophy of Nucor Corporation, particularly with respect to management-employee relations. Second are our general management methods, particularly a unique organizational structure. And third is the complete package of extra compensation, of which employee productivity bonuses are probably the most important.

Our philosophy relative to management-employee relations has four primary components. We believe that management has the obligation, first and foremost, to provide employees the opportunity to earn according to their productivity. Second, we have the obligation to manage our company in such a way that employees can feel that, if they are doing their work properly, they will have a job tomorrow. Third, employees should feel they are being treated fairly. And fourth, they should have an avenue of appeal if they feel they have been treated unfairly.

We believe that the best motivation is green. Most of our workers are unskilled or semi-skilled when they come to work for us. Previously, their earnings normally had not been high. Many have had real problems in maintaining even a modest standard of living.

With respect to job security, we feel you cannot get productive people to work nine months a year or to work for a company with a frequent history of layoffs. In addition, workers need to understand that their job security is enhanced, rather than threatened, by added productivity. This cannot be accomplished with discussions or explanations. The worker has to see over a period of years the actual results of the increased productivity before he or she becomes convinced that it is not a threat to job security. When the worker becomes convinced, the results sometimes are amazing.

Recently, at one of our divisions, we had some problems receiving approved drawings from customers fast enough to keep up with production. We discussed this openly with the production people, and we were concerned that they might slow down. Instead, the next week that plant established a new production record.

Because of our efforts in managing our business, Nucor Corporation has not laid off an hourly employee in the last 14 years.

Another key factor in the productivity improvement that we have been able to attain is the unique organizational structure that makes up Nucor.

Within our entire organization there are only five levels. Beginning at the top, you have the chief executive officer, the vice presidents, and general managers. Then you have the department manager level, followed by supervisory and professional levels and, finally, non-exempt or hourly employees. We have no assistant managers, group managers, directors, assistant vice presidents, group vice presidents, or executive vice presidents. Our lines of communications are open and informal.

Someone once asked Peter Drucker how many organizational levels a company could have before it became unwieldy. Mr. Drucker replied that this occurred with nine or more levels. At that point, he said, no young person coming into the organization could reasonably expect to move up through all the levels. Second, anyone at the top of the organization could not have any definitive idea of what was going on at the lower levels because they would be so shielded by the other tiers. Mr. Drucker went on to point out that the United States Army has nine management levels.

He also had another comment about the organization that makes great use of coordinators and assistants. "It is a symptom of a sick organization to rely on coordinators, assistants, and others whose job it is not to have a job," he said.

Nucor currently operates six steel joist fabrication plants, seven steel mills on four sites, three steel deck plants, with a fourth under construction, two standing seam deck plants, three cold finishing plants, a grinding ball plant, and a small division that makes rare earths and oxides.

Our plants are in rural areas. Many companies believe they must establish their plants in urban areas since that is where they feel the work force can be found. However, we have found the opposite to be true. Many people have a real desire to live in rural areas. However, they have had to move to cities because that was where the jobs were. Our steel mill in Jewett, Texas, is located in a county whose entire population is only 12,000. We employ nearly 500 people at that mill in a town that has a population of only 600.

When we built that mill back in 1975, we received over 5,000 applications for jobs. Most came from Houston and Dallas, from people who wanted to live in a more rural environment but who had lacked the opportunity to do so before.

In 1981, we started up a new steel mill in northern Utah in a community of 125 people. We had more than 2,000 applications for jobs at that facility. Many of these came from Salt Lake City, from Denver, and some from as far away as California.

Nucor Corporation had sales approximating $540 million in 1983, and we have in excess of 3,600 employees. Our organizational philosophy is to place the day-to-day decision making in our operating divisions. Each of our general managers is a Nucor vice president and is responsible for a division as if it were a business unto itself. With the exception of financial management, any of our operating divisions could begin tomorrow as a separate company without a moment's hesitation. Our corporate office in Charlotte, North Carolina, consists of only 15 employees, and that includes five clerical support personnel. Our corporate offices have no engineering people, no marketing people, no purchasing people.

Within Nucor, we make little distinction between various levels of the organization. All employees from the president down through the lowest paid hourly worker have the same benefit plans in areas such as group insurance, holidays, and vacation. Further, we do not have, nor do we intend to have, any company cars, company boats, or company airplanes. There are no executive dining rooms or restrooms, no company hunting or fishing lodges, and no reserved parking places. Everyone in the company including the chief executive officer flies coach.

To a large extent, the success of any incentive program depends on the degree of mutual respect and confidence between employees and management. There are times when, because of capital investment in new equipment or errors in establishing standards, the standards should be changed to be fair to the company and fair to its employees. This is a sensitive area. And it is only through mutual confidence that equitable adjustments can be made.

With any system of this type, there are bound to be occasional inequities between departments. For instance, one area may feel the other departments' bonuses are more liberal. In these cases there must be mutual confidence in the employee-management relationship to avoid serious problems.

An old saying about employee-management relations goes something like this: "Tell them everything or tell them nothing." We definitely believe in telling employees everything about the company—about its successes, about its failures, about its mistakes, and about its good decisions and its bad ones. A number of articles written about incentive programs have referred to problems created by management's reluctance to admit it had made an error in establishing standards. I wholeheartedly agree. Our approach is diametrically opposite. We make a concerted effort to convince employees that management does make mistakes. We emphasize that probably 40 percent of the decisions made by a good manager could have been better decisions. Good managers make bad decisions as well as good decisions.

When I first started to work for Nucor, President Ken Iverson told me, "John, you are going to make at least three mistakes with this company in the first few years you are with us. Each of these mistakes is probably going to cost us $50,000. I want you to be aggressive, I want you to make decisions, but I want to provide one word of caution. We don't mind your making the mistakes, but please just don't make them all in one year."

Within Nucor, management is not a popularity contest. When everyone agrees, then something is wrong. We don't interfere with every conflict. We don't create problems where there are none. Many times you have people who have small personality conflicts with others in the company, or you have people who don't agree with how the company is being administered in a particular area. That is healthy. Managements that require rigid conformance are depriving their company of new ideas, better ideas, and innovation. Worst of all, they are depriving young managers of the opportunity to learn by their mistakes.

We have four incentive compensation programs within Nucor. All of our incentive systems are designed around groups, not individuals, and here I am not only speaking of production employees, but also department heads, draftsmen, secretaries, accounting clerks, accountants, engineers, and senior officers. We are deeply committed to incentive systems. The production incentive program is certainly the most important. In that program we try to keep groups in the range of 25 to 30 people. The group's operation must be clearly definable and measurable. We believe the program should be simple, so that it can be understood readily. Bonuses should be paid promptly so that employees can directly relate their added effort and added productivity to increased compensation.

Approximately 3,000 people within Nucor work under production incentive programs. In our joist manufacturing operation, approximately 30 people are involved in each bonus group. A group covers a complete joist production line. Members are responsible for all the operations in the manufacture of joists from steel angles and rounds. This includes cutout, rod bending, rigging, tack welding, finish welding, and painting.

A group's bonus is based on roughly 90 percent of the historical time it takes to make a particular joist. If during a week members of a group make joists at 60 percent less than the standard time, they receive a 60 percent bonus. It is paid with their regular pay the following week. We simply take the complete paycheck, including overtime, and multiply it by the bonus factor. Each shift and each production line is a separate bonus group.

Each of the steel mills has nine bonus groups. Three are in melting and casting, where the bonus is based on good billet tons per hour for the week; three are in rolling, where the bonus is based on good sheared tons produced; and three are in straightening, where the bonus is based on good straightened tons produced.

Let me give you a more definite example of how the bonus works in the rolling mill and the melting and casting area. In the rolling mill, the base tons per hour varies from 5 to 11 depending upon the product size. The bonus percent per ton is 5 for the most part, with the only exceptions being the larger sizes.

In the melt shop, the base is 11 tons per hour, with a bonus of 4 percent per ton for tons over 11. To give you a quick example, if a shift in melting produced 248 good tons, the bonus would be 80 percent. Base tons for the eight hours is 8 times 11 or 88. Subtracting this from 248 you get 160 tons, or 20 tons per hour above base. We apply the bonus to all hours worked during the week including overtime.

To a certain extent we take the approach that each bonus group is in business for itself. We supply the building, the equipment, the know-how, and the supervision. But what they earn is dependent directly upon how much they produce. We do not pay a bonus when equipment is not operating. We have the philosophy that everybody suffers when equipment is not operating, and the bonus for downtime is zero.

In the joist plants and steel mills, maintenance personnel are assigned to each shift. They participate in the bonus along with the other bonus groups. The foreman is also part of the bonus group and receives the same bonus as the employees supervised.

Our rules for absenteeism are simple. We have four grace days per year. Outside of those days and the death of a close relative, military leave, or jury duty, anyone who is absent for a day loses the bonus for the week. If someone is more than a half hour late, he or she loses the bonus for the day. Needless to say, we have no problem with tardiness or absenteeism.

Under any system where the speed of production is important, the maintenance of satisfactory quality has to be considered. This is not a problem in the steel mill. You can tell by physical analysis. You can tell by the way billets roll and by physical tests whether the quality coming off the caster is adequate. This is also true in the rolling mill.

Quality is a problem in the joist plants. There we have a quality control function that operates outside the production incentive system. The inspector responsible for quality control has the right to reject a job when welds become unsatisfactory. That inspector can send the whole run of joists back to the beginning of the line and make the production group redo it. This obviously kills the bonus for the day and reduces it substantially for the week. Any group that has this happen to them once or twice is quite careful about maintaining a satisfactory level of production quality.

The production incentive program is only part of our incentive system. At the department-head level, the company has an incentive compensation program based on the contribution of the particular division in which the department manager works—or on the contribution of the corporation as a whole, in the case of department managers in the corporate office. Division contribution is defined as the profit a division earns before corporate expenses and before profit sharing. Division contribution represents a division's profits relative to the expenses it can control directly.

This bonus is based on return on assets. In a capital-intensive industry, such as we are in, that is one of the best measures of management productivity. In an operating division, these bonuses can run as high as 51 percent of an individual's base salary and are added on top of that salary. In the corporate office, it can run as high as 30 percent.

Our third incentive plan applies to employees who are not in a production function and who are not at the department-manager level. This can be an accountant, an engineer, a secretary, an accounting clerk, a receptionist, or any of a broad number of employee classifications. This bonus is also based on either the division return on assets or the corporate return on assets.

We also keep this as simple as possible. Relating back to the idea of "tell them everything or tell them nothing," we are very open with our employees in this area. Every month each division receives a report that states its return on assets on a year-to-date basis. In most of our divisions, this chart is posted in the employee cafeteria or break area together with the chart showing the bonus payout. Any employee knows the expected bonus level, therefore, at any point during the year. As I travel to many of our divisions, I can talk to employees doing work as diversified as drafting, accounting, or sales, and any one of them can tell me the level of profits their division has attained so far that year.

Our fourth program is the senior officer incentive program. Our senior officers do not have employment contracts. They receive no profit sharing, no pension or retirement plans, nor other normal executive perquisites. More than half of each officer's compensation is based directly on the company's earnings. If the company does well, the officers' compensation is well above average. Their base salaries are set at 70 percent of what an individual doing comparable work in another company would receive. If the company does poorly in a year, the officers' compensation is only their base salary and, therefore, significantly below the normal pay for this type of responsibility.

Under this program, 10 percent of pretax earnings over a preestablished level are set aside and allocated to the senior officers according to their base salary. This base level is correlated to approximately a 12 percent return on stockholders' equity. Half of this bonus is paid in cash and half is deferred.

Our incentive compensation programs are only one facet of an overall program that not only provides Nucor employees with above-average earnings, but also has several other components that help employees to identify with the corporation and its growth and profits.

We have no retirement plan. Or, more specifically, we do not have an actuarially established retirement plan that stipulates that a payment of X percent per year of service times the average of the top 5 of the last 10 years equals an individual's retirement income. That plan in turn may or may not be offset by Social Security. Rather, we have a profit-sharing plan with a deferred trust. Under this plan, 10 percent of our pretax earnings is put into profit sharing each year. Of this, about 15 percent is set aside to be paid to employees in March of the following year as cash profit sharing. The remainder is put into the trust and allocated to each individual employee based on his or her earnings as a percent of the total wages paid in the corporation.

Vesting in the profit-sharing trust is much like that of a retirement plan, wherein an employee is 20 percent vested after a year in profit sharing with an additional 10 percent vesting each year thereafter. What this means is that my retirement income and that of all other Nucor employees is going to be dependent on the growth and profitability of the corporation. Each employee receives a quarterly statement of his or her balance in the profit-sharing trust.

There's an interesting story in connection with our profit-sharing plan. We started the program in 1966 as only a deferred trust program, with no cash payout. We felt after the first couple of years that we really weren't getting much mileage out of it, probably because most employees did not really associate dollars in the trust fund as being their own. In addition, we had a lot of younger employees who were more concerned with meeting their day-to-day expenses than they were about some future retirement.

So we decided we would pay 15 percent of the profit sharing in cash. We didn't say anything to any of the divisions or employees. We made out green checks—everything associated with our profit sharing is green—and we included them along with our report about the trust fund and a certificate showing the amount each employee had in the trust fund after the increases due to investments and after the company's contribution. We noticed that, at one division, a number of these checks weren't cashed. After a couple of months we began to wonder about it. We phoned the general manager and suggested that he might talk with some of the employees and find out why the checks weren't being cashed. He called us back, laughing. He said they didn't think it was money. They thought it represented a sample check of what they might get when they retired, and they had thrown it away or given it to the children to play with. We asked him to go back and get the employees together, and he informed them that the checks were really money. He told them to go home and get the checks and take them away from the kids or let us know if they had been thrown away. We ended up issuing almost 50 new checks at that division. We don't have a problem with that any more. On the first of January, they want to know when the profit-sharing checks are going to be issued.

Another related program we have is an Employee Monthly Stock Investment Plan. Under this plan, Nucor adds 10 percent to the amount an employee has withheld from a paycheck and also pays the commission on the purchase of Nucor stock.

Another example of a positive program is in the area of service awards. Many companies give pens and pencils or belt buckles or watches in recognition of length of service, and in some environments that is appropriate. However, at Nucor we give shares of stock in the corporation. After five years of service, an employee receives five shares of stock. After another five years of service, the person receives another five shares and so on. In this way, most of our employees have become owners of Nucor Corporation.

In 1979, we established an Employee Stock Ownership Plan that increases even further the employees' ownership of the company.

A final element is what I'll refer to as an "extraordinary bonus payment." I can best explain this program by reading you a letter dated August 15, 1978:

To Fellow Employees:

Our company has a policy that all employees should share in the company's success. As part of this policy, the company contributes about 10 cents out of each dollar of earnings to the employee's profit-sharing plan. Our earnings this year are exceptionally good. Provided these earnings continue, the contribution to the profit-sharing plan for this year will be substantially higher than in previous years.

Many of us remember recent years in the past when we had problems operating at our normal levels of production because of poor economic conditions. In recognition of those difficult years and the loyalty and hard work that have made this year's performance possible, the directors have authorized an extraordinary payment. On August 15, all full-time employees who have been with the company 90 days or longer will receive $500.

I hope this payment will be a benefit to you and your family. Save it, spend it, or invest it wisely. By working together your efforts have made Nucor the finest company I know.

Sincerely,
F. Kenneth Iverson
President

This type of extraordinary bonus payment was made in 1979 and 1980 as well. The amounts and the timing have changed from year to year.

Overall, the effect of all these programs has been most dramatic. For the last ten years, we have experienced an annual compounded growth rate in sales and operating earnings in excess of 15 percent per year. The average return on stockholders' equity for United States manufacturing companies is about 10 to 15 percent. From 1972 through 1982, our average return was 24 percent. We have become the largest manufacturer of steel joists in the United States. We are the only national concern in this market, and we supply between 20 and 25 percent of all joists fabricated in this country.

In the steel end of our business, our production has increased from 57,000 tons in 1970 to slightly over one million tons in 1983. With the expansion of our Texas mill and our new Utah mill, we have the capacity to produce two million tons of steel. We are currently the tenth largest steel producer in the United States.

So much for the company. What has it done for individuals? We have a number of unique benefit plans, one of which is our scholarship plan, covering every child of a Nucor employee with at least two years service. If a student chooses to seek higher education beyond high school, he or she receives a scholarship that pays up to $1,400 per year for up to four years toward the cost.

Our company's largest steel-making facility in terms of employees is in Darlington, South Carolina. This operation employs primarily unskilled or semi-skilled workers. More than half have less than a high school education. Of the 525 employees at this plant, more than 75 percent were unskilled when hired. In 1983, the average income of the hourly employees at the Darlington mill was in excess of $30,000, significantly higher than the average annual earnings for hourly manufacturing employees in South Carolina.

Finally, and perhaps most important, our success has given all Nucor employees, myself included, a great deal of pride in our association with this company. In 1980, Nucor was selected by NBC to be included in a television documentary on productivity entitled, "If Japan Can, Why Can't We?"

In planning this program, NBC sent an associate producer to Charlotte to spend some time with Ken Iverson. I then took her to our steel mill in Darlington. In touring the mill, she had the opportunity to talk with a number of employees. We allowed her to select employees totally at random and to ask them whatever questions she felt were appropriate. One question was, "Why do you enjoy working here?" Many employees obviously mentioned that they had the opportunity to earn a great deal of money. But the universal comment made by everyone with whom she talked was that they enjoyed working for Nucor because it "was the best, the most productive, and the most profitable company that they knew."

American workers are willing to work. Too often management gets in their way. I believe we have created a management system that makes the goals of our employees consistent with the goals of Nucor.

Our employees, and I would definitely include myself in this, take a great deal of pride in being as productive as we are.

WILLIAM A. FICKLING, JR.

Succeeding by Anticipating Trends

Not a day goes by without a magazine story or television feature on alcoholism or drug abuse, executive stress, teenage suicide, or cocaine use in professional sports—to name a few subjects.

Obviously, mental health and addictive disease are hot topics in our society. In fact, they may be more than hot topics—they may be "megatrends."

Ours is a dynamic and productive society. But this means people are uprooted frequently and are subject to a variety of pressures inherent in a mobile, highly competitive nation.

These changes, experts say, have helped create a trend away from reliance on institutions and toward greater self-reliance. Ties between people and society's institutions are breaking down. This trend may have started with the decreasing importance of the extended family and ethnic groups that provided a sense of personal belonging in a diverse nation of immigrants.

For some, separation from these reference points is positive and healthy. For others, it fractures personal identity and creates insecurities and stresses that can lead to major mental and emotional illnesses or to alcoholism and chemical dependency. These are not the only reasons for the incidence of mental disorders and substance abuse, but they illustrate factors that may play a role.

What does this amateur sociology have to do with high-performance companies?

One way to be successful in business is to anticipate megatrends before they happen. If a company can get in front of a social trend, it can be there with a product or service when the marketplace catches up.

I believe our company's ability to identify fundamental changes in the external environment, coupled with sound internal dollars-and-cents decisions, has made Charter Medical successful. From our base in Georgia, we have become the number one provider of freestanding psychiatric hospital services in the world, measured in number of facilities.

To understand how we were able to mesh important social trends into our corporate strategy requires history. Our company was founded in 1969 as an operator of general acute care hospitals and nursing homes. We went public in 1971 when conditions in the capital markets were not as favorable as when the larger hospital management companies initially sold stock.

Nevertheless, we ambled along at a marginally acceptable growth rate by applying the economies of scale and the professional management techniques that were introduced to the hospital industry by our competitors following the advent of Medicare in 1966.

Hospitals are unusual businesses for several reasons. The health care consumer usually does not choose the services of a hospital, nor does he or she pay for the service directly. The patient's "purchase" decision usually is made by a physician, and the bill normally is paid by some form of insurance. In its public and private forms, insurance reimburses approximately 90 cents of every dollar spent in the hospitals of our country. The normal supply and demand characteristics of a typical marketplace have not applied to hospitals, because the public perceives no immediate connection between its out-of-pocket cost and the consumption of hospital services.

Charter Medical began operating in this unique environment. Our annual earnings growth was 15 percent. If this continued, it would have become increasingly difficult for us to raise capital at favorable rates. Moreover, it was obvious we were too far behind the others to become an industry leader.

Recognizing these negatives, we undertook a semi-formal strategy audit in the late 1970s. Four decisions came out of this process.

First, we decided to improve our efficiency and bring more revenues to the bottom line. We eliminated some overhead by consolidating certain regional operations in Macon and by cutting the number of salaried employees.

The second part of the four-part plan was to bring in new management. Charter Medical needed new blood to take the company in new directions. We made sure these executives had appropriate financial incentives, so if we were successful, key members of the management team would be rewarded.

Third, we decided to eliminate some businesses that did not fit the company's new strategic direction. We sold off our nursing homes, and we divested a shopping center and a few miscellaneous investments.

Finally, we decided to concentrate our future growth efforts in the psychiatric hospital field. There's nothing new about stress, mental illness, or alcoholism. They have been with us longer than Charter Medical, but attitudes toward these diseases and the treatment available for them have changed.

An important factor in the development of acute care psychiatric hospitals like those operated by Charter Medical was the advent of psychotropic drugs in the 1950s. They probably meant as much to psychiatry as the development of anesthetics did to surgery or antibiotics to the control of infection.

Before tranquilizers such as Stelazine and Thorazine, one-third of the patients suffering from acute schizophrenia were without hope. One-third could expect only slight improvement, with frequent recurrence of symptoms. Today, about nine out of 10 first episodes of schizophrenia have the probability of remission.

Depression formerly was a disabling, long-term illness. As medications such as Tofranil and Elavil came into use in the 1960s, depression became an illness that could be effectively treated in a two- to three-week hospital stay.

More recently, the prescription of Lithium became widespread for the clinical treatment of manic depression, a separate psychiatric diagnosis that had not responded as well to the other sedative-type drugs.

When these drugs are administered in controlled doses in the hospital environment, they allow the patient to take part in the more traditional "talking therapies" and occupational threapies that most people associate with psychiatric hospital care. Before the development of these drugs, seriously ill psychiatric patients literally could not escape their delusions or hyperactivity long enough to take part in structured therapy programs.

Once pharmaceuticals were available for the safe management of psychiatric patients, related therapies became more varied and sophisticated. These included important disciplines like family therapy and expressive activities involving music, art, dance, and rigorous physical exercise.

As people slowly became aware of the new advances in treatment, the large state institutions that used to warehouse people for their entire lives began to empty out. There was a shift toward community-based treatment—only in most instances, there were no community-based treatment facilities, except psychiatric wings or wards in general hospitals.

The freestanding psychiatric hospital offers several therapeutic advantages over the psychiatric wing of a general hospital. In the general hospital, patients are more likely to spend a lot of time in their rooms not getting any treatment. This might happen because the unit may not be staffed adequately or because there is no room or facilities for the type of comprehensive therapy programs and activities we offer at Charter Medical's freestanding hospitals.

In a general hospital, the physician might talk with the patient in his room for about 30 minutes each morning. Then there would be little for the patient to do until the doctor came by the next morning.

In our freestanding hospitals, the only time patients spend in their rooms is when they're sleeping. We have the space, the staff, and the facilities to make sure patients take part in activities or other therapy all day. Most of our hospitals have swimming pools and tennis courts for recreation. The interiors of our hospitals are attractive, with an ambience totally noninstitutional. This environment has a positive effect on therapeutic programs and is reassuring to families and visitors.

Last, in a freestanding psychiatric hospital, the psychiatrist is at the top of the "pecking order." He may not be considered part of the elite medical staff if he practices in the wing of a medical-surgical hospital. Because the psychiatrist is the head of our treatment team, he or she is crucial to our hospital.

As psychiatric hospitals became more effective, more humane, and more community-based, the old stigmas attached to mental illness diminished. Not only was the public becoming more understanding about emotional disorders, but insurance coverage became more widely available as underwriters became convinced that patients no longer were facing indefinite institutionalization for custodial care.

To sum up the three major societal factors that created a business opportunity for psychiatric hospitals: (1) The introduction of effective medications encouraged the development of improved treatment methods and therapies that made it possible to return mentally ill patients to productive society in short periods of time. (2) These improved treatment methods made huge, state-owned custodial institutions obsolete. As these patients and others turned to local community resources for treatment, there were no facilities for them. So there was an unmet need. (3) Changing social attitudes toward mental illness and addictive disease created a more enlightened environment, in which to make services available, and encouraged the development of equitable, third-party payment plans.

There were some sound business and economic reasons, as well, for adopting the strategy, in the late 1970s, that would help us capitalize on these major social and clinical trends.

First, a typical psychiatric hospital is a smaller economic unit, compared to a general acute care hospital. Because it is smaller and does not have the expensive diagnostic and surgical equipment required in a general acute care facility, a modern psychiatric hospital can be constructed for considerably less money than a medical-surgical hospital.

Second, total basic per diem charges in a psychiatric hospital are lower than in a general hospital. However, average lengths of stay are four times longer, and revenue is less dependent on the utilization of ancillary services.

Last year, 80 percent of patient revenues in Charter Medical's psychiatric hospitals was generated by room, board, and nursing services. The figure was approximately 27 percent in our general acute care hospitals.

So with less dependence on ancillary charges, the longer lengths of stay required for effective psychiatric rehabilitation do not adversely affect revenue per day. This could be the case in a general hospital, because the use of ancillary services often declines as a patient's stay in the hospital gets longer.

On the cost side, psychiatric hospitals are less labor-intensive than a general hospital. Two employees per occupied bed are required to operate Charter Medical's psychiatric hospitals. In one of our typical general acute care hospitals, that number is closer to four employees per occupied bed.

Although revenue is lower in psychiatric hospitals, both variable costs and fixed costs are less. When you take the net and spread it against a significantly smaller base of assets and equity, the returns in a psychiatric hospital are sometimes better than in a general hospital. This was a crucial consideration for Charter Medical when we did not have much money. But it is still an important factor today.

Third, psychiatric hospitals provide the opportunity for more extensive marketing. Because of the nature of mental illness and addictive disease, fewer patients present themselves for treatment than in physical medicine.

Most general hospital referrals come from physicians. The potential referral base of psychiatric hospital services includes schools, courts, pastors, private psychologists, counselors, family members, and loved ones.

People frequently will intervene on behalf of a mentally ill individual who won't seek help himself. This aspect of mental illness expands marketing opportunities, provided marketing and advertising are done with dignity and a desire to educate. We employ television and other mediums in advertising extensively.

We concluded that developments in the external environment, primarily advances in psychiatric treatment, would create a viable business opportunity, if we could make the internal organizational changes necessary to put these theories into practice.

At this time six years ago, Charter Medical had five psychiatric hospitals, all of which had been acquired. Today, we operate 27 freestanding facilities in 12 states and London. This is more hospitals than any other company.

We have 17 more psychiatric hospitals under construction or development, including facilities in five new states. We are operating 11 general acute care hospitals and one specialty surgical hospital in seven states, plus a new facility to open in Macon this year.

Over the past five years, our revenues have grown at a compound annual rate of 30 percent. Net income has increased 42 percent per year compounded, and earnings per share have increased 41 percent. Five years ago, our capital expenditures were $20 million. This year we expect to spend $107 million on new hospital construction.

One of our yardsticks is return on equity, which was 9 percent in 1976 and 30 percent in 1983. One major goal was to become an industry leader in return on equity.

I am sure anyone from a high-performance company would say luck is involved in achieving extraordinary business success, and Charter Medical is no exception. But we must recognize extraordinary rewards usually come only at great risk, and there's a difference between taking a business risk and managing that risk.

The most efficient organization in the world will not prosper if it has a product or service no one wants or needs. By the same token, the best idea in the world will not succeed if it cannot be delivered to the marketplace in an efficient, quality way.

We have tried to make our own luck whenever possible. We determined a strategy based on our best analysis of a number of external and internal factors and stuck to that strategy. We found a niche in the health care business where we had a chance to become a world leader.

Charter Medical made a long-term commitment to the psychiatric hospital business. We believe any company that intends to be viable over the long haul must pay attention to the quality of its service.

Charter Medical's psychiatric hospital strategy has become more of a day-to-day tactical challenge for management. We are looking strategically at ways to improve the understanding and treatment of mental illness and addictive disease, not only in our hospitals but through education and awareness programs.

MARK C. HOLLIS

Motivating Employees through Stock Ownership

Perhaps the best place to begin would be to share the story of how Publix Super Markets' well-known slogan, "Where Shopping Is a Pleasure," came into being. It was the brainstorm of a young Bill Schroter, now vice president of marketing for Publix, who had been hired in 1949, fresh from the University of Florida, to reorganize the advertising department. Soon after coming to work, he chanced to read the book by Marshall Field, *Give the Lady What She Wants*. The title epitomized the Publix spirit, and within the book Bill came across an idea that applied directly to his work. Beware, warned Marshall Field in discussing advertising and slogans, of patting yourself on the back, calling yourself the world's biggest, the world's best, etc. Slogans, he advised, should offer a promise rather than a praise of self.

Bill then took a hard look at the ad he had been preparing. The layout included the Publix slogan then in use, "Florida's finest food stores." He knew that it had been started by Publix founder, George Jenkins, years before. But it was self-congratulating and offered no promise.

Bill mused over this wording for some time, and he kept hearing the comments people made about shopping in our stores. "Publix is such a pleasant place to shop," was an expression heard frequently. Or someone would say, "The people are so pleasant." These customer comments triggered something in Bill Schroter. He went in, with a certain amount of trepidation, to talk to Mr. Jenkins about Marshall Field's advice. He gulped a couple of times, told him the present slogan was contrary to this advice, and then showed him his new idea, "Where Shopping Is a Pleasure." And so it has been ever since.

Since that day, this slogan has been used, without alteration, in every ad and sign in every store. Yet our success is due, not to a catchy and popular slogan, but rather to our commitment to make that slogan (and its partner "Where Working Is a Pleasure") a part of our philosophy. With this company philosophy as the basis of my remarks, let me move on to answer the most frequently asked question about Publix: "How did you do it?" You already know something of our financial success, so there is no reason to take time here to detail those figures. Let's get right to the answers.

Perhaps the first answer some might give would be our location. All 275 stores are in Florida. I certainly don't have to remind anyone what has been and will be happening to Florida's population growth. When and if Florida stops growing (or slows appreciably), we may have to look for growth in new areas. But right now our sights are set on keeping up with the Florida market and expanding our share of its business.

A second reason is our conservative financial management. We are one of America's largest retailers totally owned by company employees. Until 1976, we never paid a dividend. All profits were plowed back into the business and were used to open new stores, update equipment, build new support facilities, and keep our company modern and efficient. Today our dividends represent less than 15 percent of our earnings. We have an extensive program of expansion and renovation that will be financed with depreciation and earnings.

Third is our progressive expansion program. We opened 11 super-markets in 1983. We will be opening 12 to 14 more this year. Each store will be approximately 39,000 square feet.

Just as important is our commitment to keep our existing stores up-to-date. Over the last several years we have been expanding 10 to 15 stores a year and refurbishing and remodeling 15 to 20 stores. As we look around at some of the U.S. chain stores that have experienced bad times, we frequently see sad neglect of their existing stores. A company that places all of its efforts on new stores alone will be in big trouble in years ahead.

The fourth answer to the question of why we have been successful is our commitment to high standards. Recently, at a meeting with clerical employees from several stores, I asked why they thought Publix had enjoyed such success. One of their answers was, "Because we have made a commitment to high standards." I asked them to be more specific, challenging, "What standards are you talking about?" They replied, "Customer service, high-quality products, good housekeeping, and sanitation."

I think they are right. Publix has continued to expect these high standards to be carried out in its stores. We believe, and we have convinced most of our people, that the customer is the most important person in the store and that if we do not please the customer, there is no need for our store. If we give better service; if our people are friendly and helpful, the customer will want to come back again and again.

We believe that customer loyalty is earned by good customer service. A store may gain some temporary advantage by offering cheap prices, but long-term loyalty comes from customer service. The same philosophy holds true for quality products. Generic labels and low-quality, cheap, private-label merchandise may be popular for a while, but will not produce long-term customer loyalty.

We were one of the first companies in America to experiment with prepackaged meat and, later, prepackaged fruits and vegetables. One of the first lessons we learned in prepackaged products is the absolute requirement for careful control of quality. The customer must develop confidence in the product.

This philosophy has been carried out in more recent developments with our milk and ice cream plant. Our customers have come to expect the Publix label to be top quality.

High standards of housekeeping and sanitation are also important. The consumer associates food purchasing with food preparation. Therefore, clean floors, clean shelves, and clean packages are important to the customer. We all know that and we accept it as a necessary ingredient in the food merchandising program. The important question is, "Do our employees understand it?" In my opinion, our employees must be convinced as much as we are that housekeeping and sanitation are vital to our success.

Our fifth reason for success is our ability to maintain our flexibility. The supermarket is a fast-moving, fast-changing, highly competitive business. Anyone who is going to be successful must provide the structure and the training that will allow management people at the lowest possible level to make decisions necessary to meet the latest competitive maneuvers.

When visitors come to Publix, particularly visitors from West Germany, they always want to see our organization chart and our policy manual. They are confused when told that we have neither. We believe our management people should be interested and involved in all areas of the company. We do not want them to restrict their interests to the narrow area that might be described in an organizational chart.

Certainly we have some company policies and some of them are in writing. But we do not have a policy manual. We do not want our store managers and our supervisors to think they are so restricted that they cannot make a decision without consulting a manual. I do not suggest that this approach is right for everybody, but it has worked well for us at Publix.

A sixth reason that I offer for Publix's success is a commitment to stay in our own field of expertise. This, of course, is contrary to the philosophy of some other highly profitable companies that have achieved remarkable success by branching out into new ventures.

George Jenkins, our founder, made a decision many years ago that our commitment was to be to the retail grocery business. We wanted to be the best food merchants in America. He felt that we could not accomplish this if we were also trying to be the best furniture dealers, or the best clothing store operators, or the best pharmacists, or the best in general merchandise. Consequently, when you visit a Publix store, you will see a traditional supermarket.

Another factor that contributes significantly to our success is our firm policy of promotion from within. All but four of our officers have worked their way up through retail stores or through our warehousing and distribution system. Those four officers have special skills such as accounting or real estate. Young people joining our company as stock clerks or in warehousing know that, if they work hard and develop their skills, they too can enjoy opportunities to move into bigger and better jobs.

Finally, and most important for our success, are our people. The expression "our people are our most valuable asset" has become almost a cliche in the industry today. But we should note two things about a cliche: (1) it contains an element of truth, something worthy to take note of, but (2) it has been repeated so often that no one listens any longer. Cliches often become empty rhetoric, devised to impress some group.

With that in mind, I repeat, "Our people are our most valuable assets." Through fair wages and a good benefit program, we have been able to attract some bright, enthusiastic, hardworking, and ambitious people. But that's only half the job. The other half is to keep them and to motivate them continually.

Financial incentives are but one method used for motivating employees but, in my opinion, not the most effective. We share our corporate profits with all full-time employees through a profit-sharing retirement trust plan. We also pay a cash bonus to retail employees based on the profits of their stores. We issue 40,000 shares of Publix stock to the employee stock ownership trust plan each year, and this year we will be making an allocation through a tax-credit employee stock ownership plan.

Of even greater importance is the fact that we have been successful in convincing our people that we are interested in them—not just as employees or numbers on the payroll sheet, but as real human beings. We care for them. We are truly concerned that they find their place of employment to be where "working is a pleasure."

This attitude toward people is contagious. They feel this good attitude toward them, and they transmit the same concern to our customers. We believe the customer-employee relationship that exists in our company is a unique and powerful force that works for us to stimulate both sales and profits.

There is yet another reason for our success that I have intentionally set aside. That is our use of and dependence on technology. The rate of technological progress continues to stagger the imagination. But we must not be deceived by this amazing technology. No matter what wonders the scientists may perform with their machines, their computers, and their robots, the success or failure of business will still depend, as it always has, upon the magic quality of "manpower," by which I mean human power. Manpower, with its brainpower, its muscle power, and its heart power, continues to be the most critical factor for success.

It has not changed a great deal since that great American industrial leader Andrew Carnegie said, "Take away my factories and my plants; take away my railroads, my ships, and my transportation; take away my money. Strip me of all these, but leave me my people, and in two or three years I will have them all again."

Why is Publix the place "Where Shopping Is a Pleasure"? Because it is also the place "Where Working Is a Pleasure."

ROBERT STRICKLAND

Sustaining a Tradition of Excellence

Let's focus our thoughts on what the concept of excellence should mean and the significance this plays in operating a successful business.

In addition to financial data, a recurring theme runs through most of the annual reports and annual stockholder meetings regarding the importance of people, the challenges posed by deregulation in many industries, the intense competition in all, and an awareness by corporate managers of the growing need to reach for new levels of achievement.

Questions each of us have to ask ourselves in our individual situations are: How much of this corporate prose is merely rhetoric and how much is reality? How much is gloss and how much is substance?

Introspection, now and then, as to how we perceive ourselves and our companies—and how others perceive us—can be a useful exercise. You have to make your own evaluations.

Every business possesses distinctive characteristics. Companies excel in different ways: by manufacturing a better product, by rendering a better service, by using better marketing techniques, by delivering a higher degree of customer satisfaction.

We can agree there are some fundamentals cutting across the whole spectrum that can help us determine how well we are doing. These "givens" include such basics as integrity, honesty, truthfulness, fair dealings, and high moral standards. These qualities are not debatable or negotiable. Either you have them or you don't. If you don't, you have no business being in business.

When we talk about "sustaining a tradition of excellence," we are looking at a combination of three ideas. It is impossible to quantify these concepts, except that each has its effect on the bottom line. First, "sustaining" suggests continuity. Second, "tradition" is history. Third, "excellence" says you're doing something better than average.

Tradition implies that you have been around for a while. Our company is fortunate to have a rich heritage dating back to 1891. Those of us in senior management today can take no credit for the company we inherited. The credit for our tradition belongs to those who came before us.

The many leaders preceding us at Trust Company were good bankers and community builders, with a sense of commitment to operate their business on high principles and to excel in every way possible. Their dedication shaped our corporate character and reputation.

We in management today have the responsibility for "sustaining" these traditions. This heritage provides us with definite guidelines specifying the way decisions are made and things are done. We are doing our best to maintain this legacy, so we can pass on to our successors a company as strong or stronger than the one we inherited.

That leads into the concept of "excellence," which has many elements. We believe the foundation for excellence begins with operating a sound company. In our business, that means abundant capital and a strong, clean balance sheet. It means an insistence on high quality in all that we do—first-class facilities, state-of-the-art equipment, and a full range of financial services delivered on a profitable basis. It means high quality in our loan and investment portfolios and a generous reserve against contingencies. As an example of our own conservative approach, we have classified as nonearning certain of our Latin American credits similar to those many others have yet to recognize as nonperforming.

We may be more conservative in our dealings than some, but that in no way rules out aggressiveness in developing and maintaining strong, close relationships with individuals and businesses in our target markets. We want to do business with those who expect and appreciate value-added service, delivered in a superior manner.

Excellence means committing a significant amount of resources to research and planning, to ensure we have a firm handle on changes in our industry.

We intend to be fully competitive in traditional and emerging financial services where we have the experience, the ability, and the capacity to perform well and where we see opportunities to realize a reasonable profit.

The element of risk is inherent in banking. But excellence, to us, means avoiding unnecessary risks or situations that could give us a short-term gain but would impair the long-range strength of our company.

Underlying these objectives, we intend to excel in recruiting, training, motivating, and rewarding the people of our organization. We want to develop bankers who are professional in every way and who measure up to our standards of performance. Our future depends on the quality of fresh talent in our company. We look for high achievers—bright young men and women who someday will be able to take over where we leave off.

Another element of excellence, to us, is in the area of community involvement. Our company has always felt a corporate responsibility to invest a portion of its financial and human resources to enhance the communities in which it operates. It is simply a matter of self-interest to give support and leadership to ensure an atmosphere conducive to a healthy business environment.

Excellence also means continuous attention to detail, a dedication to the work ethic, and a challenge throughout the organization to strive for increased personal productivity. When you put these elements together, they find their way to the bottom line.

The two most commonly used measurements of bank performance are return on average common equity (ROE) and return on average assets (ROA). We had a 1983 ROE of 24.38 percent and an ROA of 1.58 percent. These results, coupled with a five-year compound earnings growth rate of 28 percent, place us high among all major banking companies in the country.

We at Trust Company take pride in this performance, but we constantly remind ourselves that it's easier to get to the top than it is to stay there. The first question most bank analysts ask us is, "What do you plan to do for an encore?" That brings us back to earth in a hurry.

We don't have any secrets or magic formula at Trust Company to explain our performance record. This has resulted from a combination of hard work by many people, clearly stated and widely understood goals, determination, plus some good luck.

Several years ago, we established a sharply defined corporate objective to become a top-performing banking company. Most major decisions made since the mid-1970s have been considered with this in mind.

Each new year means another encore for all of us, if we intend to remain in the forefront. To me, our ability to perform a quality encore is the greatest challenge we face as managers. In golfer's language, I guess this could be summarized as: "Keep your head down, keep your eye on the ball, and use plenty of follow-through."

BERNARD MARCUS

Educating Managers and
Employees

Delores W. Steinhauser, Moderator

We have heard a great deal about productivity through people. I think that's a testament to the fact that these companies live and breathe those ideas. They know they can leverage their hard assets through their soft assets and get tremendous productivity gains by treating people with respect, giving them the right incentives and the right motivation to perform.

Now we'll look at innovation and how to stimulate it, and at entrepreneurship—going out with a vision, starting a company, and building something from that concept.

Kathryn Eickhoff said it's not the giant Fortune 500 firms that are producing economic growth and employment growth in the United States, but the entrepreneurs—those who start companies with fewer than 20 people—who are producing the real growth today.

Six years ago, in 1978, there was no such company as the Home Depot. Today, the Home Depot employs 2,400 people, whose lives have been affected by the vision of a group of entrepreneurs. The company has $250 million in sales after just six years, and it makes a 15 percent return on assets in an industry where the norm is typically less than 5 percent.

This group of entrepreneurs envisioned a better way to serve an industry. That industry is the home-improvement industry, the do-it-yourself movement. Through their concept, they were able to reduce prices and offer a higher level of service. What better combination can you conceive for serving your fellow man?

It's also the typical entrepreneurial action-oriented company.

When we visited them, Bernie Marcus was leading us around the corporate headquarters. We were lagging behind, about five or six steps, because he was walking briskly down the corridors. He turned the corner and looked back, but we weren't there. He stopped and said, "You'll have to hurry up, this is retail." That typifies the energy level and the excitement that goes on at the Home Depot.

Marcus will be followed by Thomas Jacobsen, senior executive vice president of Barnett Banks of Florida; Eugene Epstein, senior economist for the New York Stock Exchange; Alan Kantrow, associate editor of the Harvard Business Review; *and Rosabeth Moss Kanter, author of* The Change Masters.

The rapid growth of the Home Depot's business has proven to be a surprise, even to us. When we first opened the Home Depot stores, we anticipated a maximum of $8 million per store in retail sales annually. Instead, we are now averaging over $18 million per store. This year we may have stores that will reach $30 million in sales. To our knowledge, there's nothing like it in this industry, in the United States, or in the world.

Why has the Home Depot been able to do this? One of the reasons is our method of training our managers and personnel.

Today, one of the most obvious things about retailing is the lack of trained, motivated personnel. Think about your own experience of walking into a store and either being ignored by the sales people or having to deal with people who are not knowledgeable about what they are selling and who really don't care if you buy.

Unfortunately, every business today has this problem. In banking, there are too many tellers who don't care. The banks that are doing well are the ones that have people who care and are highly motivated. To the same extent, the retail companies that are doing well are the ones that carefully train their staffs.

From the moment we started this company, we were determined to be different. We resolved to have people in our stores who were well-trained, highly motivated, aggressive, and concerned about the customer. Every retailer will tell you this is what he desires, and most will tell you about programs they have started to accomplish this.

But at the Home Depot we don't just talk about it. We live it. Everybody in the company, starting with the chairman of the board, is a trainer and a teacher. And if someone is not a trainer and a teacher, we will teach him or her how to be one. Our company has grown from zero volume to $256 million in just five years. We expect to reach $500 million this year and $1 billion in the near future. But we can accomplish this only by training our people correctly.

Most important, we select the right person for the job. To begin with, our interviewing process is crucial. Before a manager hires anyone, he must be sure the individual is honest, can be motivated, and, to be successful in the retail business, is an extrovert who enjoys talking to people. Fully 90 percent of the people who work in our company work at the store level in a selling capacity, so this is an important quality to look for.

As a result, we accept approximately one out of 10 applicants. Most people are not suited to our business, so we don't want them working for us. If someone doesn't like people and doesn't care to talk to people, why have that person represent us? To have the right person, we've got to hire the right person in the first place.

There is another aspect to this. Think about hiring people who go through six months of training before they can become productive. What happens if we then find out they don't represent us properly? We have to start the whole cycle over again. Before we know it, it's cost hundreds of thousands of dollars. In a company our size, that figure may be millions of dollars. That's why we spend a great deal of time determining who to hire at the outset.

In our company, every manager and assistant manager goes through an extensive training program. Nobody starts at the top. We never hire a manager and put him in charge of a store. We don't care what his experience is. We don't care what his salary level is. We don't think there's a manager available in the United States today, in our business or in any business, who is qualified to run our stores until he or she is first imbued with the Home Depot philosophy. Therefore, everybody who comes into our company starts at a lower level and goes through a three-and-a-half-month training program.

For example, we recently hired an in-house attorney. He's going to represent us in EEOC (Equal Employment Opportunity Commission) cases, in liability cases, and in labor cases. But in order to understand our business, he has to work at the store. So he started out unloading trucks. Our philosophy is that everyone starts at the bottom and learns the business from the bottom up.

We have two assets in the company: inventory and personnel. Each of our stores carries $4.5 million to $5 million worth of inventory and a staff of between 125 and 160 employees. Of these two assets, the inventory is easily controllable; the asset that's a variable is personnel.

That's why one of the most important people in our company today is the director of personnel. He's a vice president and has a great deal of power. His job is to develop and train our people.

In the training process, each employee goes through a planned procedure that is followed and graphed very carefully. Each new employee is rated and charted. We talk to them as they progress, and we counsel them. We also discuss their observations about our business. We get some interesting observations this way. In fact, we invite criticism of our business. We're not in love with our own mistakes. If we can change them, we do.

After our new employees complete the initial training period, they are put into a program that is more formalized. We have a tag program, in which we identify people for future growth. We see a special opportunity in the development of young individuals, so we follow their careers from an early stage.

Those tagged for potential advancement are given the opportunity to enter a management training course. We conduct a training session at the main office three times a year. We bring in every manager, assistant manager, and individual we have targeted for future growth. It doesn't matter if that person is a salesman in the lumber department or the electrical department, or loads cars outside. These training classes are taught by the key officers of the company: the president, the executive vice president, and the financial vice president. We do all the training ourselves. We don't hire outsiders to train our most important asset.

In this course, we teach our basic business: what the Home Depot concept is and what we expect from our workers. We try to motivate them. We try to get them as excited about our business as we are.

And what do we teach about the home improvement business? We teach newcomers that we represent the one asset that over the last 30 years has proven to be the most important asset the American people have—housing. You may not need a new dress, a new toy, or a hairdo, but everyone needs a roof over his or her head. Along with food, housing is the necessity of life that people cannot do without.

We also emphasize the current economic volatility in America. We point out that interest rates have gone up and down, inflation has gone up and down, and the economy as a whole has gone up and down, but the value of a home has continued to go up. The home has become the one asset that people have that is worth the most, and we are in the business of helping them protect that asset. We show people how to improve that asset. We imbue our workers with the philosophy that they are in a necessary business, that they are doing something worthwhile. Once we get them to understand this, they can go out and represent us properly.

The last meeting we hold with new employees is called the "chairman's meeting." It's conducted out in the field, in smaller groups of about 15 to 18 people. For these meetings, we travel to the stores, to the workers' home ground. These meetings are designed so I can listen to what these employees have to say. I cannot overemphasize how much money this company has saved because of those meetings, by making our workers participants in our business, listening to them, and reacting to their suggestions.

Think of all the people out there representing us who see things happening day after day that we can't see any more. They come back and tell us how to make our business better. Our reaction time on credible, feasible suggestions is almost immediate. If a meeting is held on a Tuesday and a suggestion makes sense and will save money, then we react to it on Wednesday. By Thursday it's a company policy.

Our employees have seen this happen over and over again. They now know that the company reacts to them. They feel they're a part of the company, and it gives them the motivation, the esprit de corps, that helps us grow. It is obvious what's happened. We've gone from zero to $256 million in five years.

On top of everything, we follow one principle that is important: consistency. We're consistent in how we treat our people, and we're consistent in how we evaluate performance. We are also consistent in our rewards—our managers are eligible for bonuses based on a return on assets, something they have control over. And we are consistent in the way we listen to our people. As a matter of policy, we allow our employees to have forums with management, so we can react to what they say. We don't just go through the motions.

I believe that going through the motions is the worst thing any employer can do. It frustrates your employees and discourages them from wanting to work for you. It strips them of their enthusiasm. We believe most people honestly want to work hard and want to produce, and don't want a feather bed. That's our experience.

Before we opened the last group of stores, 52 percent of our employees were shareholders in this company. That means they have confidence in this company and they're willing to invest in their own labor.

We think the Home Depot will continue to grow. We're opening 6 to 10 stores this year. Next year, we'll probably open 15 to 20 more. We hope one day the company will be a national firm. We're building for it. We have people in training in all of our stores. In the future, we probably could open 5 to 10 times the number of stores we're now opening each year. But we won't do it. The Home Depot will not open a store unless it has the kind of employees it wants to staff it.

THOMAS H. JACOBSEN

Innovation through Experimentation

I'll begin with a brief background of our company's position 20 years ago and outline how we evolved to our current asset size in excess of $11 billion. Using that evolution as a backdrop, I'll discuss the Barnett management process, planning, the structure of our organization, control systems, and leadership. Then I'll describe what we see as the driving forces in the environment—deregulation, technology, the economy, and our competition in the Florida market.

Within this framework, I'd like to talk about innovating through experimentation at Barnett. First of all, I'll describe the kind of environment that facilitates experimentation and, second, why innovation is so important.

Let me give you some general background. In 1940, Florida had 1.9 million residents and ranked 27th in population in the United States. In 1980, the state had grown to 9.8 million and was ranked seventh. By 1990, with close to 1,000 people a day moving into Florida, we will have 12.5 million residents, and we will be fourth in population, passing Ohio, Illinois, and Pennsylvania. By the year 2000, Florida should have 14.8 million residents. Perhaps we'll pass New York and be third.

We've got a tremendous economic force at work in our state, and we have but to position ourselves to take advantage of that force. We're not a bank that needs to go to Argentina or Europe for business. We want to stay in our own marketplace and do what we know how to do well.

Twenty years ago, Barnett was a relatively small banking organization in northeast Florida with five banks and $200 million in deposits. In addition to our headquarters in Jacksonville, we had locations in St. Augustine, DeLand, and Cocoa. Ten years ago, we had grown, primarily through acquisitions, into 18 counties. We had acquired a bank in Dade County (Miami), in Fort Lauderdale, in Palm Beach, and other areas, and we had grown to $1.7 billion in deposits. Five years ago, we had expanded further, into seven more counties, and had begun to fill out a statewide franchise, again primarily through acquisitions. By that time we had achieved a deposit level of $3.1 billion.

Since then, we have more than doubled that figure, and we're looking at doubling it again in 1984. Our assets at the end of 1983 equaled $9.4 billion. As I mentioned at the outset, our assets currently total more than $11 billion, and we should achieve $12 billion by year-end, counting acquisitions.

Barnett is now in 37 counties containing 93 percent of Florida's population. Earnings in 1983 were $81.9 million, a 1 percent return on assets, which is the midpoint of our target range of between .90 and 1.10 percent in a growth market.

If Florida leveled off in terms of growth, or if Barnett positioned itself as a nongrowth company, we believe we could improve profitability by something in excess of 20 basis points on assets. However, we think the correct strategy now is to reinvest to capture future growth. We are doing that, and our market share now stands at a record 14.43 percent of all commercial bank deposits in the state.

Currently, we are either number one, two, or three in 32 of our 37 counties in terms of market share, and we have the largest, most complete banking franchise in Florida. Barnett also is the premier consumer lender and the largest construction and commercial real estate lender in the state. We have high asset-quality controls and the full array of products associated with large banking organizations. We're a low-leverage bank; that is, we use mostly core deposits for funding. We don't buy funds extensively in the money markets, and we don't position ourselves to work with thin spreads.

Now allow me to shift focus and describe what we call the "Barnett management process." We feel that managing change effectively is the foundation that facilitates innovation and experimentation. For that reason, we continually emphasize the importance of the planning process. Each spring we conduct a careful environmental scan; we prepare a source book, assess our competitive position, and record changes year-by-year. Out of this reassessment comes a mission statement from which we articulate specific, quantified targets. To reach these targets, we develop strategies against the backdrop of our position in the environment. Each strategy may require thousands of tasks to implement.

Let me share with you some of the targets we have designated in the last year or two. These are specific goals in deposit market share, consumer banking, corporate banking, regional expansion, noninterest income, productivity—which is especially important to us—delivery systems, and support resources. And finally, let's consider some specific financial targets.

First, by the end of 1988, let's say we have targeted our total deposits to be equal to at least 10 percent of the deposits in all commercial banks and savings and loan associations. The deposit market was $97 billion at the end of 1982. The thrifts had about half of that amount, and the banks had the other half, with Barnett accounting for $5.8 billion. Let's assume that the total deposit market is expected to grow to $191 billion by the end of 1988. If Barnett grows at 15 percent compounded over five years, our deposits will increase to $11.6 billion. Since 10 percent is $19.1 billion, we would have a $7.5 billion shortfall. That implies a need for aggressive acquisition activity. Various strategies come out of that targeting that constitute the basis for our heavy acquisition activity in Florida.

Another Barnett goal is to maintain or improve our position as the premier consumer banking organization in Florida. We are the leader in core deposits, consumer loans, and total real estate, and second in residential real estate. This has implications for how we define our structure over the next five-year period.

We want to be the premier corporate bank as well. Our market share of commercial and industrial loans is above 9 percent. To be the premier bank, we must surpass 15 percent. The strategies that flow out of that goal dictate that we add people in corporate banking at the corporate staff level and in the individual banks who can mount an active calling effort on our target markets.

Moving to another goal, we know that noninterest income will constitute a larger proportion of our profitability in 1988 than in 1982. It's not going to compensate completely for any secular squeeze in our net interest margin, but it's going to help.

Actually, we feel the only way to compensate effectively for any squeeze is to become more productive. To accomplish that requires substantial capital investments. Technology takes a while to implement, so if we don't start now, we will be unable to compensate.

Delivery systems and resources to support a bank that will grow into the $20 billion to $25 billion range over the next five years will require a different orientation to data processing than that of a bank which is not growing.

We know that reregulation will bring some increase in our capital requirements. We also know, on the other hand, that we'll have deregulation opportunities with additional financial services. So we're innovating in some of the technology areas that require less capital.

We're planning to maintain or enhance existing support resources in anticipation of achieving an asset size of $23 billion in 1988. For this, as I mentioned, we have made enormous capital outlays early in the time cycle, and we expect to get significant productivity initiatives later. We're stepping up activity in our large computers and doing some things in our technical areas that will allow us to become more efficient in the next three to five years.

Finally, our 1988 financial target is to remain a leader in return on assets, in compound earnings-per-share growth, and in solvency statistics such as primary capital-to-assets. We want to use the liquidity derived through the money-market accounts by increasing our loan-to-deposit ratio. These targets imply that we have to achieve a balance among earnings, profitability, and growth. If we see earnings and profitability eroding a bit, we'll slow our growth activities. We're not looking for other business outside of our marketplace to compensate for any slowdown in earnings. We will simply slow our growth to pick up the profitability and the earnings in our market.

Briefly, that might very well be the essence of our plan. It's well-defined with known parameters, and we do it every year. We create a profit plan within those parameters, and we draw up tactical plans and task lists in the fall and early spring. We believe this is a crucial element in the effective management of change. Without it, innovation through experimentation would be random, haphazard, dangerous, and potentially ill-fated.

Now, let's turn to our structure, which sets us apart from other banks in Florida. First, we have a portfolio of banks that includes a $2.5 billion bank in Miami and $1 billion banks in Tampa, Orlando, and Jacksonville. In the other communities, our banks range in size from $25 million in assets to a $1 billion bank in Palm Beach County.

Each of these affiliates has its own bank president. We firmly believe it's important to have senior people close to the market. Senior people with proper incentive will innovate, and successful innovation in banking, we believe, must be market-driven.

We manage each of the banks differently, according to what the market will give us. Our high-profitability banks are mostly in relatively slow-growth areas in the northern part of the state. The higher profitability of the northern banks allows us to expand in the southern region where there is greater growth potential.

Tight control systems have been designed and implemented in recognition of the differing banks. The systems are all-inclusive and tailored to the individual characteristics of the affiliates. The attribute that allows us to manage change is the commonality of the systems. The controls include Management Information Systems (MIS) by function, financial control systems by line item, and market control systems by product and by market segment. Most important, we have a peer group orientation. Every bank's information is available to every other bank, which engenders a lot of competition.

We target profitability, earnings growth, and market-share gains for each affiliate, and we manage our banks accordingly. Experimentation is triggered by earnings or growth pressures and carries with it visible, tangible opportunity for short-term payback. The leadership style that embodies all of this is extremely entrepreneurial, with a high energy level. We're close to our customers. We have tailored management with a market focus. Our presidents can earn up to 50 or 60 percent in incentive compensation over their salary base in some banks. The bank presidents and their senior people in the affiliates are innovating all the time, because they have, first of all, the freedom to do so, and, second, they have the appropriate incentive—the bottom line. Incidentally, all of our banks are relatively autonomous and, at this point, doing well.

That's what we call the Barnett process. Now, I'd like to turn to the variables in the environment, where we see a number of driving forces. These include government, technology, the economy, and financial institutions in the Florida marketplace.

We experiment heavily in the area of technology. We started in 1976–1977 with automated teller machines (ATM) on a prototype basis in Jacksonville. We expanded that service slowly when we were at the break-even point on transactions. We have continued expanding the service throughout Florida, and now we have 215 automated teller machines deployed. That number will be close to 300 by the end of 1984.

The Honor System is a statewide electronic switch connecting essentially all the automated teller machines in Florida. We were one of the founders when that was started in 1983. We expect the Honor System to be the largest ATM sharing activity in the world by the end of 1984.

We're also without peer in our cash management activities. In 1978, we created TeleCheck, a cash-flow affiliate requiring little capital. It's a check verification service that has grown to 20 offices throughout the Southeast, with between 10,000 and 15,000 merchants in the system. In 1984, we'll make in excess of $3 million with this affiliate.

We're doing the same thing with Barnett Brokerage Services, a discount brokerage activity we started last year. We did $100 million in volume in 1983, and in 1984 we'll do 30,000 to 50,000 trades and should break even.

We first experimented with our credit card operation 10 to 12 years ago, and now it is one of the largest in Florida. It has $400 million in outstanding balances and 425,000 cardholders.

In-home banking has been in the news lately, and we're right in the middle of that development, working with Automatic Data Processing (ADP) on a prototype. We're also beginning to work with Knight-Ridder in Miami. We think this will be an important delivery system in the future and in the next six months to a year we expect to begin real innovation that will make us dominant in the field statewide.

Actually, everywhere you look, Barnett is innovating with new technology, from the automated clearinghouse and automated teller machines to TeleCheck and cash management. We think other income and productivity gains to be derived from such innovation are extremely important to the future of our banking organization.

Now I'd like to take a look at various high-performance factors from a financial focus. It's important to make the distinction that in these areas we make no claim to high-order innovation through experimentation. We just don't think there should be any volatility or uncertainty injected at this level. We believe basic, fundamental banking works every time.

The issues in banking this year are earnings consistency, asset and earnings quality, capital strength, and growth momentum and potential. What we've done in terms of earnings consistency is grow from $23.2 million in 1978 to $81.9 million in 1983. As to earnings quality, we're at the top of the list in terms of nonperforming assets when compared to our peer group. Reserves are held to 1.3 percent with conservative charge-offs. We have engineered up to 40 percent excess capacity in our data processing area. This allows us to assimilate acquisitions comfortably with stability, and it allows us to innovate. With tight control systems in the production area, we have no trouble experimenting with technology.

We also have a solid tax base. We write off all acquisition expenses, and we have conservative intangible amortization policies in market-extension acquisitions. We write off software expenses, and we recognize all benefit expenses. So we have what we think is high earnings quality.

In the area of capital, too, we are very strong. Equity-to-assets, for example, is at 5.46 percent, compared to the Keefe 24-Bank Index figure of 4.96 percent.

Our primary capital-to-assets is even stronger—123 basis points over the regulatory target. We deploy capital judiciously for acquisitions and investments in technology.

There are some stock valuation factors that we also think are important. Generally, Barnett's performance has been recognized in the market. Our shares, which traded in the 20s back in 1980, reached a high of 42 3/8 in 1983. Sun and Southeast, our principal competitors, were roughly in the same trading position in 1980. They haven't advanced as much as Barnett.

Taken together, then, what are the elements of Barnett's total performance equation? Our strong, and in some respects unparalleled, competitive position in the Florida market today is the foundation. Out of that we focus on proactive planning and strong controls. We have a unique structure and highly motivated management close to the market. This emphasis on managing change recognizes the dynamic, even volatile, environment in which deregulation, technology, and competitive pressures are the driving forces. And finally, we adhere to stringent financial targets, never forgetting that our overriding focus is the bottom line.

These are the elements of the equation, which implies that a change in one triggers a change in others. We believe Barnett's equation is in equilibrium. It is dynamic; the elements change month-to-month and year-to-year, and the interdependencies change accordingly.

In summary, let me pose the question, "Where and how much do we innovate through experimentation?" The answer is that we innovate a lot. We experiment at the affiliate level. We also do quite a bit with technology because we think, over time, we'll have a secular squeeze on our net interest margin. If that happens, profitability will drop unless we compensate through other income and, more important, through efficiency gains.

We've functioned in this way for the last five years and have experienced a dramatic surge in growth and earnings. We will continue to do so in the next five years, and we would expect the same level of performance.

Audience Member: Mr. Jacobsen, would you care to comment on your asset-liability management system?

Thomas Jacobsen: We have an asset-liability committee that was created to manage the company's profitability targets. It is constituted of the senior people in the corporation and meets regularly to price liabilities and set policy on tax issues, gaps, and mix. This group also discusses at some length the merit of new financial instruments.

We do not intentionally mismatch across the balance sheet. We are slightly liability-sensitive in the 0–90 day range, and, because of the surge in money-market accounts, we are about 5 percent liability-sensitive over six months.

Our general philosophy is to take our earnings out of the market rather than try to anticipate which way interest rates will move. The Florida market is growing at double-digit levels, and we are trying to match that.

We use a computerized model that forecasts various components of our financial statements, and we do extensive sensitivity testing, particularly for interest rate projections.

EUGENE EPSTEIN

Innovation and Economic Growth

Imagine this is the year 1785 in the United States. Our capital stock includes such items as wooden plows, draft animals, wagons, slow-moving sailing ships, hand pumps, Franklin stoves, and primitive printing presses. Now perform a mental experiment on this economy: assume the rate of capital accumulation quadruples and innovative activity stops permanently. What happens to the pace of economic progress?

With the benefit of hindsight, we know the negative effects would have been incalculable. The cotton gin would not have been invented, the iron plow would not have been introduced, and, of course, such things as railroads, clipper ships, and blast furnaces—not to mention trucks, airplanes, and assembly lines—would barely have been dreamed of. There would have been a tangible increase in material well-being, but nothing remotely compared with the progress that actually took place.

I chose a distant period in our history for this exercise only because the results are so dramatic. But it would be instructive to rerun history according to these rules for a more recent era—the years since World War II. Imagine that we experienced a vastly accelerated rate of capital accumulation but with no change at all in products and processes since 1945. Our lives as workers and consumers would not approach the world of today.

Now try a different mental experiment. Imagine Ruritania, a mythical country with a high standard of living whose physical capital embodies the most advanced technology. Imagine that because of some inexplicable disaster Ruritania's capital base disappears overnight. Citizens wake up one morning to find all the country's factories, offices, and stores vaporized. In other words, Ruritanians are now at a stage of economic

The views expressed in this chapter, adapted from a recent speech to a conference held by the Federal Reserve Bank of Atlanta, are not necessarily those of the New York Stock Exchange.

development that places them far behind even the poorest of third world countries. But then something surprising happens: so rapid is Ruritania's economic advance that, 20 years after the catastrophe, the country's material well-being is restored to its previous level.

How could this happen? If you're tempted to question it, consider that this mental experiment is not purely hypothetical. Think of Germany and Japan, whose industrial cities were reduced to rubble during World War II. Twenty years after the war ended, these countries had achieved levels of prosperity exceeding their own prewar levels, as well as those of countries whose capital base was relatively untouched by the war's devastation. The inherent advantage Japan and Germany had was the "knowledge base" embodied in their people. Just as with Ruritania, this proved more decisive than a capital base.

In fact, the postwar "economic miracles" in Germany and Japan have caused some people to suggest a reverse fallacy about the consequences of physical devastation. These people say Japan actually benefited from the destruction of its factories, because this freed it to build new factories with the most advanced technology. We can be happy these same theorists never suggested the U.S. government dynamite its country's factories to boost economic progress. Even if such a catastrophe occurred, the innovative know-how embodied in the mind and spirit of our people would bring recovery soon enough.

THE NATURE OF INNOVATION

The first mental experiment asked us to assume vastly accelerated capital investment without innovation. The result was disappointing. The second asked us to assume full knowledge of innovation but with all the fruits of past efforts at capital investment destroyed. The results suggest that when it comes to faster economic growth, innovation plays a primary role.

Innovation is not quantitative. A quantitative boost in capital simply means increasing the number of plows, hand shovels, and calculators available for productive use. A quantitative boost in labor means increasing the number of hours people work—either through more people working, or through the same people working more hours, or both.

These quantitative factors are of relatively minor importance to economic growth. Of much greater significance is the *qualitative* factor of innovation. A qualitative boost in capital means installing a better plow, hand shovel, and calculator—or, of course, replacing these with tractors, steam shovels, and computers, that is, with capital that does the same job better. A qualitative boost in labor means people working smarter with the capital they have. As a practical matter, working smarter is always required with new capital; computers would be worth little without people trained to use them. Even with capital that is familiar and established, there is plenty of scope for people to work more effectively.

Finally, innovation means something else—something that poses difficulties when we try to quantify economic growth: not just better inputs in the form of capital and people, but new or better consumer products and services—money-market funds, supermarkets, Tupperware parties, video recorders, personal computers, and extended-wear contact lenses. An increase in economic growth conjures up a vision of more of the same products, when what may really be going on is that products and services are new or getting better. As a practical matter, factoring new products and services into those magic numbers that chart growth in gross national product (GNP) is more an art than a science.

THE QUALITY OF INPUTS

All the empirical studies economists have done of the sources of economic growth confirm the conclusion we have drawn intuitively from our mental experiments: What counts most in boosting growth is not the quantity of the inputs but the quality. For instance, economist Simon Kuznets writes in *Modern Economic Growth*, an empirical study of both developed and underdeveloped countries: "[My] inescapable conclusion is that the direct contribution of man-hours and capital accumulation . . . hardly account[s] for more than a tenth of the rate of growth in per capita product—and probably less. The large remainder must be assigned to an increase in efficiency . . . due to the improved quality of the resources, or to the effects of changing arrangements, or to the impact of technological change, or to all three." According to Kuznets, the role that innovation plays matters far more than the quantitative increase in worker-hours and physical capital. Other investigators, including such productivity experts as John Kendrick and Edward Denison, have come to the same conclusion.

A MATTER OF PRIORITIES

None of this is meant to imply that capital investment does not matter. Even Kuznets acknowledges it makes some difference—and other investigators place a heavier weight on it. Also, it is artificial to say capital investment plays a certain role and innovation plays another. How can we put new technologies in place without capital investment? The real point as applied to today's economy lies elsewhere: more than anything else, faster economic growth requires an increase in innovative activity.

From 1960 to 1969, the annual rate of economic growth was 4.4 percent, and the percentage of GNP devoted to investment in new plant and equipment (called the investment ratio) averaged 9.9 percent. But from 1969 to 1979, we got only a 3.1 percent rate of growth from an investment ratio of 10.5 percent. In other words, in the 1960s we got a more substantial payoff in economic growth from a lower rate of investment. Since 1979, the investment ratio has hovered close to 11 percent.

The crucial question is: How much would it matter if, all other things being equal, we could boost the investment ratio to 12 or 13 percent, a level the U.S. economy has never before achieved? No doubt this would bring an increase in growth. But according to anyone who has done an empirical study of the subject, it would matter much less than boosting the "investment payoff" through an increase in innovative activity. If the 1960s are any guide, it is possible to return to something like a 4.4 percent rate of growth even with no increase in today's 10 to 11 percent investment ratio.

These priorities are worth emphasizing for a number of reasons. To begin with, certain economists and policymakers have an unfortunate tendency to reverse them. As a result, they have called for solutions that would do more harm than good. For instance, one group of respected economic thinkers believes that in order to boost growth it is necessary to tighten our belts. Their reasoning is simple: An increase in economic growth requires an increase in the investment ratio. In order to find the resources for this increase we need a decrease in consumption. A *Business Week* economist has written with male chauvinist flair that "the U.S. economy is in the position of a once svelte and beautiful woman who has allowed herself to turn into a blowsy balloon and must therefore go on a rigorous diet. For an economy, just as for a fatty, restoration of health requires drastically reduced consumption." Lester Thurow has written that "some Americans will have to accept a decrease in their own share of the GNP for several years, if more of it is to go where it will do the most good in the long run." He writes that the big question is, "Whose standard of living should be trimmed?"

I find something offensive in these demands for widespread sacrifice. They remind me of the kind of five-year-plan mentality prevalent in those bureaucratized economies we call socialist. Market economists should know better, particularly if they bothered to read the findings of people who have actually investigated the sources of economic growth. The majority of Americans have trouble paying their bills to begin with. To impose greater sacrifices on them in the name of economic progress is irresponsible at best. Not that I would object if the investment ratio were to increase—but only if it happened voluntarily. Nor is it necessary for people to cut their consumption in order to increase the investment ratio. Increases in capital investment might come out of future increases in consumer income or out of government expenditures via lower taxes.

I counter Thurow's question about trimming living standards with two of my own: Where are we to find the energy and imagination for a decade of innovation? And what can the government do to permit the market economy to unleash these energies?

RIGGING THE FINANCIAL GAME

This leads to the second reason for deploring the emphasis of investment over innovation: It deflects attention away from measures that could make a difference. In particular, it makes it harder for us to focus on the real ways government policies distort the allocation of capital funds. In order to maximize the rate of innovation, the market game has to be fair. People and companies with the most profitable ideas should have a reasonable chance to secure financing. But when government policies rig the game, innovative activity is likely to be stifled.

One misallocative policy to be reformed is the double taxation of corporate profits. Approximately 25 percent of all capital investment comes out of reinvested corporate earnings. Much of that money probably is being misallocated. The reason is that the tax structure gives investors a powerful incentive to reinvest earnings in the corporation that produced the earnings rather than to seek alternatives. Take an investor in the highest bracket, whose dividends will be taxed at the 50 percent rate. Now say that the investor would like to take some of the earnings from his or her holdings in Company Y and invest in Company Z. But the only way to take the earnings out is in the form of dividends. If the investor does so, 50 percent of the capital funds will already have been taxed away. So the tendency will be to allow the originating company to keep and reinvest the earnings, even if its profit potential is inferior.

The government should tax each corporation as though it were a partnership among shareholders. This would mean abolishing the corporate income tax and making each taxpayer fully liable for his or her share of the corporation's profits. This would remove the shareholder's tax shelter on reinvested earnings. Whether a dollar of the corporation's profits was reinvested or distributed as dividends, the tax consequences to the shareholder would be exactly the same. Shareholders would then have an incentive to consider all alternative investments on an equal footing. The result would be that innovative companies would have a better chance of competing for funds.

It is also worth mentioning the harm done to innovation by tariffs, import quotas, loan guarantees, subsidies to business of all sorts, and barriers to entry imposed by "old-style" regulation. Whatever these policies achieve, there is no question they serve to misallocate both capital and labor. If you prop up nonviable companies, you will give them access to capital and labor that could go to other, more viable companies.

Of course, there could hardly be an objection if there were both an increase in innovative activity and an increase in the investment ratio, so long as this resulted from voluntary decisions to save. But if the past is any guide, the first approach is more feasible than the second. An increase in innovative activity would mean a return to the recent past while an increase in the investment ratio from present levels would mean radically departing from it. If economic scholarship is any guide, boosting the quality of the inputs matters more than boosting their quantity. From the standpoint of both public policy and public understanding, the issue is a matter of emphasis.

> *Audience Member*: I have a short, simple question. How does an innovator get through to those who have the capital?

> *Eugene Epstein*: You'd get through more easily if some of those government policies that favor the corporations were altered.

> *Audience Member*: You've been talking about innovative ideas. It seems imbued in our society that those who have the capital assets are reluctant to invest at a greater risk ratio.

> *Epstein*: Perhaps you should ask the 600,000 people who started new corporations in the past year. They apparently were able to convince people to take the risk. That is a perennial problem of perception, just as we all feel we're underpaid. Innovators and entrepreneurs all feel they're denied access to capital.
>
> In the 1960s, many people must have felt that way. Yet we still achieved a substantial rate of growth and a substantial rate of innovation. I think we're likely to have it again without any substantial increase in investment.

> *Audience Member*: If I understood you correctly, you referred to the steel companies as lacking an entrepreneurial attitude, being reluctant to invest capital in new plants. I differ with you, because they've had to put millions of dollars into pollution controls that generated not one additional ton of steel. Yet their competitors in Taiwan, Japan, and other countries have not had to spend this money. I'm not saying we shouldn't have required those antipollution modifications, but I differ with how you said it.

> *Epstein*: I accept that modification. Let me note that macroeconomists have also said that you really can't look at the investment ratio because there was so much investment in pollution-control equipment. This was a statement made by the Joint Economic Committee of Congress. In fact, if they had bothered to look up the figures of the Commerce Department, they would have found that there was a good estimate for the amount of antipollution equipment companies had to install. Even if

you subtract that from the overall investment rate, though, you would find the investment rate was up.

You're certainly right that the steel companies and other U.S. companies have been hobbled, at least to some degree, by the need to put in that kind of equipment. I was only saying that if the established steel companies had really wanted to go to the capital markets, they would have found a willingness to lend money to the large steel companies. That was the point I was making.

Alan Kantrow: Let me try to respond to that last question about funding sources for new technology. Today's venture capital industry didn't exist in anything like its present form 15 years ago. If you talk to the leaders in that industry, they will tell you that now there is too much money chasing too few deals. The money is there. There are also R&D partnership dollars coming out of programs conceived in the Commerce Department, largely under the sponsorship of Bruce Murrifield, the undersecretary for science and technology.

A lot more project lending has also begun within American industry. If you're an old-fashioned steel company, for example, and your bankers are unwilling to lend you a lot of money to finance some new technology that you need, they might be willing to lend to the project—if the *project*, and not the overall standing of the company, is the security. We have begun to see that kind of project lending in some of the higher tech areas.

The large, full-scale, full-line steel producers looked at major new process technologies for years and wouldn't touch them, even when they had the money, or could get the money, to do it. Continuous casting had been around for years as a proven technology before the major companies started to buy into it. Basic oxygen furnaces had been in existence for a long time before some of the big guys started to buy in.

ALAN M. KANTROW

America's Industrial Renaissance

Four major characteristics, in my judgment, seem to be associated with the companies that are most productive, most far-seeing—those that have really managed to get their arms around what it will take to succeed in the 1980s and beyond.

I don't want to discuss particular kinds of business decisions. I do want to discuss attitude and viewpoint. I believe very deeply that what really characterizes excellence is the viewpoint of the people at the top and throughout an organization—how they view the world, how they see things, what their assumptions are.

During World War II, as Elting Morison tells the story, a British field artillery unit wasn't getting the rate of fire from its gun that it was supposed to get. There was one artilleryman who discharged the gun, one who loaded, one who aimed, and two who stood around. Just before the gun was discharged, these last two would snap to attention and stand there, immobile. About a second or so later, they would come back to an at-ease position. No one knew what they were doing. It was not a very efficient way to do things. It just didn't make sense. But the field commander wouldn't change it, because that was the way they'd always done things.

Some puzzled officers went back and asked all these people, "Why did you do it that way?" No one knew. So they asked some time and motion experts to do a study, and they couldn't make any sense of it. They finally were reduced to the expedient of taking a movie of the operation and showing it to anyone who might have an idea what this was all about. Finally, an old retired officer said, "I know what those guys are doing who are snapping to attention just before the gun is fired—they're holding the horses."

Might I suggest that, in a broader sense, an awful lot of what goes on in American management is one or another version of "holding the horses." The insidious thing, of course, is that the assumptions on which you operate when you're doing that seem so reasonable, so self-evident, so straightforward, and the reinforcement you get about them is so consistent and clear, that you have no reason in the world to challenge them. It's like wearing a pair of glasses so long that you forget you have your glasses on. You look through those lenses so consistently that you forget there's something between your eyes and the world out there.

The first point I want to make, then, is that the good companies—the companies that are succeeding today and give real promise of doing well in the future—have given up holding the horses, are able to see the world as it is, and are doing what is necessary to adapt.

They understand, for example, how the competition in their industries has changed from what it was as little as a decade ago. The thing that is still hard for some people to grasp is that the competitive world has fundamentally shifted. The arena of competition in industry after industry is quite different from what it was in the recent past, and the likelihood that things are ever going to go back to the way they were (no matter how fondly we might wish for it) is minimal.

We hear much talk about how high technology is going to save us and how old manufacturing industries are dead or dying and should be quietly buried. The implication is that the best thing we could do is adopt a kind of corporate "living will" policy—death with dignity: Let's not watch U.S. Steel suffer, let it go, we don't need it, we don't need its employment. Biotechnology will save us all.

That is nonsense, but what it masks is a notion that somehow high-tech industry and older manufacturing industry are fundamentally incompatible. But if you've ever actually been inside a computer plant, you know that much of what they do is old-fashioned metal bending and assembly. If you've ever been inside an automobile plant or a modern steel plant, you know that there's quite a lot of pretty spiffy-looking high-technology stuff going on.

No one would characterize the Home Depot as a high-tech business, or the home-improvement industry as a high-tech industry. As Bernard Marcus said, his company's most important asset is its people. But there's no way in the world those people could manage the Home Depot's inventory without a pretty sophisticated computer system. If that's not high technology, I don't know what is. It's managed well, that's clear, but it just doesn't make sense to say that business is a sleepy little old-fashioned mom-and-pop operation, grown large. It's not. It may be in an industry that is nonsexy by some standards, but it sure has a significant high-tech component. If that component didn't work well, Home Depot wouldn't be doing as well as it is at the moment.

The world has changed in that there is no safe preserve in the American economy for nontechnology-based businesses in industries open to international competition. The categories—high tech and low tech—are misleading, and the good companies understand that. High-tech companies, if they're going to succeed, also have to be excellent manufacturers. Perhaps IBM's greatest competitive strength, after its brand franchise and reputation for service, is its reputation as a responsible, high-quality, low-defect manufacturer. And it understands that. When it floated that huge debt issue some years ago, it took most of that billion dollars and put it into manufacturing plants.

The second thing that has changed is obvious and fundamental: We now exist in a universe of global competition. The American domestic market for years was a safe preserve for American companies. The market was rich; it was virtually infinite. It could buy everything we could possibly produce, and foreign competitors were just a blip on the horizon that didn't matter. That world is gone for good.

American companies know only too well that the domestic market is not a safe preserve any more. They're beginning to understand that, if they are going to survive long-term, they have to learn how to compete better at home and to sell and produce abroad. Many, many industries have become global. That trend is unlikely to reverse.

The companies that have managed to get their arms around the way the terms of competition have shifted also understand that competing on the basis of excellence in manufacturing is critical. After World War II, we went through more than a decade and a half where competition on the basis of marketing was just about everything. The automobile industry for years competed on the basis of styling and marketing and little else. You stamped sheet metal a little bit differently year to year; you raised or lowered a tail fin; you painted the metal differently—and that's about all you did.

If you went to buy an American car in 1965, there was not one single piece of technology on that car that had not been available for sale in the American automobile market 30 years before. If you go into a dealer's showroom tomorrow, you'll find that statement simply doesn't hold true any longer. The same thing has happened in a variety of industries. Competition based on marketing (in the sense of styling and fashion) has increasingly become competition based on excellence in manufacturing, with a high-technology component.

If you had gone to buy a car in 1910, you would also have been faced with a range of choices that might have surprised you. You could have bought a car that was open or closed. You could have bought a car with three wheels or four. You could have gotten a steering wheel or a tiller. You could have gotten a car fueled by gasoline, or diesel fuel, or electricity, or steam. And, again, if you had walked into that proverbial showroom in 1965, that range of choices simply was not available to you. In fact, Lee Iacocca, when he was still at Ford, is famous for having told his people, "Give the consumers leather, they can smell it, that's what they want." He doesn't talk that way anymore. Neither does the industry.

What had disappeared, in terms of the technical variety of products in the market circa 1960, has begun to come back now in a major way.

In 1980, if you took two comparably equipped subcompact cars, one U.S., one Japanese, and after you accounted for shipping costs and freight costs and insurance and everything else, the Japanese producer could put his car on a dealer's lot anywhere in the United States for between $1,500 and $1,800 less than the American producer. This is a car that sold for about $5,000 or $5,500, and that $1,800 is a conservative number. It assumes a currency exchange rate even less favorable to the Japanese than is the case today.

That's an immense difference. It's not because the process equipment of the Japanese is more extensive. That doesn't explain it. In fact, the capital intensity of Japanese automobile companies is substantially less than the capital intensity of their American competitors. Nor is their equipment newer. Nor is it all based on sophisticated new "star wars" technology. The difference really lies in the way their whole manufacturing process is managed—the sheer efficiency of their operations.

We have seen—in two comparably equipped engine plants—the Japanese turn out twice as many engines in the same amount of time. That is not money or technology or new equipment. That is management. And we cannot compete with it unless we are willing to compete on those terms. That has changed. That is something new.

We can't stress quality strongly enough. We have learned at great cost that not only is quality important, in terms of its value in the marketplace, but bad quality is phenomenally expensive. We used to think, in industry after industry, that quality was very expensive, that you paid so many dollars and you achieved a certain level of quality. Every increment beyond that, we thought, became more and more expensive. Certain levels of quality were unaffordable. Not so. It turns out that the better the quality, the cheaper the overall costs (including scrap and rework) long-term. An immense amount of research in a variety of industries has shown that.

Dave Garvin, a professor at Harvard, conducted a study of the room air-conditioner industry in the early 1980s. For every 100 air conditioners that rolled down American assembly lines, 63.5 defects were discovered in the plant. This does not include defects discovered under first-year warranty out in the field. Now, some of the American operations that make room air conditioners are independent companies, but some are divisions of rather famous, well-known industrial corporations. These were not fly-by-night operations. In Japanese plants the defect rate was a mere .95.

Here's something even more troubling. When Garvin went to the

Japanese companies to gather data, they already had the information. The most recent figures were literally posted on the factory walls. Yet when he went to the American companies, many didn't have the information or know how to get it, and he had to spend a lot of time trying to reconstruct it from their own data.

Today, companies can't stay in business if they proceed like that. The nature of competition has shifted in such a way that excellence in quality is of prime importance, not only because it is essential to establish and hold a customer franchise, but also because it is essential as a means of controlling the overall efficiency and productivity of an operation.

Still another way competition has shifted is an increased emphasis on rapid product development. Many American companies, which for years have pumped lots of dollars into corporate research laboratories, have had great difficulty getting the fruits of their research out of the lab and into products. Perhaps the best example of that is Xerox's Palo Alto Research Center (PARC) in California. Years back, the chairman of Xerox made a very farsighted decision. He said that sometime in the future we're going to need to know everything there is to know about digital technology. We know nothing about it now, he said, and so we'd better start a research center and learn everything we can, so we'll know it when we need it. And they did it.

This center has absolutely lived up to its billing. Unfortunately, very little of the technology developed there has found its way into Xerox products. It has found its way into products that other people make. Xerox was simply not structured internally in such a way that it was able to absorb—or thought it important to absorb—this new technology as it was being developed. That was the way the system was geared.

The Japanese understand all too well that when you start looking at technologies and markets that are new, as opposed to markets that are extensions of old markets, or technologies that are extensions of old technologies, traditional market research can't tell you everything you want to know.

In the years after World War II, when IBM conducted a market research survey of the worldwide demand for mainframe computers, the answer came back that the total possible demand for the next five years was a hundred or so units. When Xerox did its first market research on the demand for office copying machines, it was told that the market was tiny, because the only people who might buy a copier would be large insurance companies and certain government agencies that process lots of paper.

It's relatively easy for consumers to tell you what they like or don't like about products they understand. It's very hard for them to tell you what they like or don't like about things they've never seen before. The only way you're going to find out is to put the products, or some temporary version of them, out in the market and see how it responds. That's what the good Japanese and American companies have done all along.

The Japanese understand perfectly well, for instance, that they don't know what the most important applications of high-tech ceramics are going to be. All they know is that they're not going to find out by sitting around in a room and asking each other; they know they're going to find out by putting applications of that technology out in the market and seeing how consumers respond—and learning from that response.

Sony's Betamax, which started a huge business, was introduced to the market several times before it was finally introduced successfully. The first Toyota cars exported to the United States lasted about three hours on California highways and then died. One can imagine that most American companies would have been unwilling to stay with these projects and absorb the continued long-term costs.

The notion that product development is a long-term effort marked by failure along the way has been foreign to many of us. But the good companies understand it and are acting on it. It is critical, and the companies that don't recognize its importance stand less of a chance then they might in the years ahead.

Management of people also is important. You should look at a firm's work force as a huge reservoir of human capital, not as reservoir of costs to be cut back whenever possible. It is simply not true that the efficiency of Japanese plants comes from people wearing funny uniforms, singing songs, and doing exercises. Nor do people who are halfway intelligent believe that such shenanigans will work in American companies.

We know what to do. You know how you would like to be treated working for an organization. This is no mystery. But the notion that we actually have to buckle down and do it comes as a surprise to some American managers. The good managers understand it and have been doing it for years. The others are simply going to have to learn it or go out of business. It's becoming that clear.

The new terms of competition demand a focus on productivity. However, there is an immense danger in such a focus at the company level on productivity improvement and enhancement. The danger is this: In most operations, there is fat to be trimmed, there is slack to be gotten rid of, there is overhead to be cut back. Cost efficiencies that fat and lazy managements never felt the need to address before are now essential. These cost-savings opportunities, of course, need to be addressed. But if you take only a narrow view of productivity improvement—only a cost-reduction–efficiency view—after a certain point you're locking yourself into a dead-end proposition. If your focus is limited to constantly increasing efficiency, you're locking yourself into doing the same thing better and better. The problem is that you are progressively removing the possibility of building in flexibility, building in the capacity to adapt, building in the capacity to restructure the operation—building in the ability to do things differently, not just do them better.

For instance, perhaps the greatest advantage offered by the automated process technologies now available for factories is that they make possible a huge amount of flexibility, on the factory floor, which had never been there before. It begins to be the case that you no longer can achieve production efficiencies only through the high-volume, standardized production of commodity-like items. Typically, in the mature phase of industry competition, you need to compete on the basis of price. You want high volume, you want a standardized product, and you want to make that product in huge batches that begin to resemble, as much as possible, a continuous flow of operation. Then, when someone comes in with a nifty idea of how to process the whole thing differently, you have to say, there's no way we can do this, we have too much invested. You have locked yourself in.

No matter what flexibility-oriented rationalizations have been given for buying robots, they are being used in simple cost-reduction applications. When those returns begin to peter out, as they must, a lot of chairmen are going to be looking at their manufacturing specialists and saying, "You told me to buy into this stuff, and we put up a lot of money, and it is not worth it, and I want your hide." An overly constrained sense of what productivity is can prematurely narrow the needed flexibility and needed adaptability of an organization.

A well-known phenomenon in industry, called the "sailing ship phenomenon," demonstrates that when industries come under challenge from new technologies, their first response often is to try to do better the things they're already doing. When sailing ships began to be threatened in the mid-nineteenth century by steam ships, we saw the greatest burst in sailing ship technology we'd ever seen. All of the early returns from that burst were positive because sailing ships got a lot better. But still they were not good enough.

The greatest burst of development in vacuum tube technology came after the transistor was introduced. But it wasn't enough. The most rapid advances in turboprop engines for aircraft came after the introduction of the jet engine. Again, it wasn't enough.

The inclination to do better what you're already doing locks you into the past in a way that can be disastrous, long-term. But the early returns tend to confirm the course you've chosen, because you're showing results. You're saying, "We are getting more out of our research, we're selling better, things are doing better." No one sees the edge of the cliff; all they see is the good return. It can be insidious. Beware.

The final item about this narrow view of productivity is that we have to look at what our companies do internally, not as a collection of bits and pieces, but as a system where all the parts fit together. It makes no sense to maximize the productivity of one piece, if that's going to create a bottleneck down the line. It doesn't make a whole lot of sense, for instance, to do wonders with your utilization of labor if that labor feeds a bottleneck in your plant. The whole system has to work together, and it can lock you in, if you take a too narrow view of productivity. Adapting to the new terms of competition and avoiding a too narrow view of productivity are crucial.

A third point is to be wary of the conventional wisdom, even if it is taught by experts or by prestigious organizations. For instance, we all know, don't we, that the best thing in the world is high market share? Consultants have been telling us this for years. They have been saying, in effect, "Get high market share at virtually any cost." Well, the non-sense is plain, of course, because there are ways to get high market share that will put you out of business tomorrow. The notion seems to be that, if you have high market share, then other things will follow. Indeed, a lot of research shows that companies with high market share seem also to be the companies that post good profits. True enough, but the question for managers is how to get there from here—and at what cost.

An equally insidious notion involves traditional cost accounting systems. If these systems ever bore any relationship to what actually goes on in a plant or a factory, they don't now. They were derived at a time when direct labor comprised the vast majority of manufacturing costs. That situation has been turned on its head. These systems bear no relation to reality today. We desperately need new accounting systems. We need better ways to understand our costs. And we need methods that reflect what's actually happening today, not what the situation was 60 years ago.

In this regard, American companies have in the past tended to be rather slow in developing their own in-house process capacity, very reluctant to build their own equipment, very ready to license it, or sell it—whatever they had.

What we find is that, if you're going to stay in the game and be good, you really need to understand your process. You need to understand your product, and the best way in the world to do it is to be the master of your own process. You must have some in-house competence at system building. Otherwise, not only are you vulnerable to your suppliers and vendors, but you don't really understand what you're managing. It's absolutely critical to get away from the notion that managers simply manage collections or portfolios of assets. That is not what managers do. Managers manage people, they manage products, they manage projects, they manage systems, and they manage production lines. They don't manage abstract sets of assets, and if you think of them only as numbers on some abstract balance sheet, you don't know what you're doing. The good companies understand that. Of course you need formal financial reporting and control systems. No one argues with that. But that is no substitute for hands-on, nuts-and-bolts knowledge of what you're managing.

A final point—essential to success now and in the future—is getting beyond the notion that industries, like biological organisms, go through a life cycle that is irreversible. There has long been abroad in the land a notion that industries are born, they go through a rapid growth phase, they become older and mature, they throw off cash, and finally they wither and die, and there's nothing you can do to resuscitate them. Once they're gone, they're gone, according to this theory. And if you put more resources into the industry, what you're doing is throwing good money after bad. So we get the "write-them-off" mentality. As a general rule of behavior, that's nonsense. There is enough evidence now of what's happening in the country to make us consider very, very seriously the possibility that we can reverse that drift toward maturity. It's not academic theory. In an awful lot of cases, it is, indeed, happening.

If you had asked 20 years ago which industry was most like walking death, you would have had a choice between shoes and railroads. Yet the only major part of the railroad industry in this country that is not getting truly revitalized today is the part the government owns. What about shoes? Massachusetts used to be the world leader in the shoe industry, which for years was treated as if it were not only dying, but as if it were already dead. Yet the shoe industry has now become high-tech. Think about what's happening in athletic shoes and outdoor-wear shoes, in the application of new materials, new modes of fabrication, and physiological analyses of foot movement. That industry has just absolutely been turned on its head, and more changes are coming. Yet it would have been written off 10 or 15 years ago by lots and lots of people.

U.S. Steel doesn't seem very eager to be in the steel industry. It wants to be in the oil industry. Nucor does want to remain in steelmaking, and Nucor is making money. At Harvard, I once was sitting next to a man I didn't know, listening to a third person talk about how the steel companies couldn't hack it and might as well close up shop. Why did the U.S. need a steel industry anyway? This man beside me stood up and said, "Well, that's very interesting, but it so happens that I run a small steel company down in Texas, and we are more efficient than any Japanese producer, and we are just about as efficient as the best Korean producer. That makes us one of the best in the world, doesn't it?" The name of the company was Chaparral Steel.

A number of smaller, tightly focused steel companies are using the best available technology and managing their people well. Chaparral, for instance, is doing some fascinating things in managing its foremen, a problem that few companies have ever really tried to address.

The automobile industry is another example. The huge reorganization that you see going on at General Motors is part of it. The great resurgence in Ford's quality is part of it. It *is* happening.

In the 1960s, you could stand on a rooftop in New York City and see a forest of TV aerials and say, "The consumer electronics industry is mature." There were, however, a few folks in Japan who didn't buy that and absolutely turned that industry upside down. That sort of thing has happened in case after case. When she heard that Governor Thomas E. Dewey of New York was running for president a second time, Clare Boothe Luce dismissed his chances by saying that a soufflé never rises twice. That may or may not be true about American politics. But when that kind of soufflé notion gets applied to industry, it is not only misleading, it's downright dangerous. It's nonsense, and we have to get that purged out of our heads.

Be wary of taking too narrow a view of productivity and efficiency. You should distrust the conventional wisdom about things like market share or cost accounting, and you certainly should not believe that life cycles are irreversible and that, once one reaches a mature state of industry competition, all is lost. Those are the essential changes in management thinking we're going to need if our companies are going to do well in the future.

When it comes to the fate of our industry, the one thing that we have learned in the last couple of years is that abandoning experience in favor of untested assumptions—holding the horses—can kill us.

   Audience Member: Perhaps industries don't have life cycles, but would you say that, instead, occupations have life cycles?
   Alan Kantrow: I didn't say that industries don't have life cycles. I said the argument that those life cycles are irreversible and one-directional is not true.
       Of course they have life cycles. The problem is that, when we look at industries, we see they go through some process or sequence of development. That process has characteristics that differ from industry to industry. It's a general phenomenon. The metaphor locks us into a way of thinking, which might not apply to a specific case.
       I'm saying that if you are a manager and you think you're in an irreversible, mature phase, and your boss feels the same way, are you going to put a whole lot of money into capital investment? Are you going to worry about doing much more than harvesting profits? What you do is harvest money like crazy to feed other things.
       Edward Jefferson, the chairman of DuPont, said that one of the research investments on which they made the greatest return was an investment they made in nylon long after it had

become a mature product. They improved it a bit, and they turned it around. They had a huge run for the money.

Here 's another example. Procter and Gamble's Duncan Hines unit is now in the process of making and selling prebaked cookies.

The problem with all ready-to-eat chocolate chip cookies is that they are hard, all the way through, because of the crystallization of the sugars. Nonetheless, cookie makers for years have built their plants near local markets and maintained a separate fleet of delivery trucks to fight a losing battle to get these cookies on the shelves before they go hard.

It turns out that, if you improve the technology in the cookie-making process, you can produce cookies that are crusty on the outside but still chewy inside. You can produce them in one plant, and you can distribute them through the normal channels you use to transport all the rest of your products to warehouses and supermarkets, and absolutely change the economics of the industry.

Now I don't think you would have told me 10 minutes ago that the chocolate chip cookie market in the United States is a vibrant, vital, high-growth market. You might have said that although it's a sizable market, it's not one with a lot of life. But that's not true. These little changes can have huge competitive effects. Some industries, of course, will die. It happens. Yet we need to look carefully on an industry-by-industry basis before writing anyone off.

Audience Member: Do you think that our government should provide subsidies to encourage industries with bright prospects?

Kantrow: I'm not big on the government's ability to pick winners and losers. I don't think government knows more than the managers do. I do think, though, there are circumstances in which it makes sense to give temporary help—whether it's a subsidy, a temporary import restriction, a temporary rollback of pollution regulation, or other such things.

The problem with the way the government has done it in the past is that it has asked nothing in return. The best example is the steel industry. The steel industry has been a protected industry for a long time. It has been shielded from foreign competition in most of its markets, and it screams about the ones where it is not protected. For years the industry did very little in return. For the most part it did not modernize. The companies that did modernize were slow to do so. Many did not use the grace period to retrofit their plants, to bring in new equipment, to do good things with their management of people. That strikes me as overwhelming policy idiocy. I don't think the government's role should be to restrict joint research in the name of antitrust. That is nonsense. The companies are much better than the government guarantor against R&D activity becoming collaborative and collusive in restraint of free trade. The companies don't want collaboration on development activities. That's when it becomes proprietary. But, the expense of doing basic research has grown so astronomically that the companies can't always do it on their own. Only the big guys can really undertake major research on their own. That's one thing the government can do.

Audience Member: Would you have tried to save Chrysler?

Kantrow: I'm not sure what I would have done with Chrysler. I probably would have done what was done, but I would have monitored it more closely. As I understand it, Chrysler met few of the intermediate reporting requirements that had been imposed. The Federal Trade Commission didn't do a good job of staying on top of that. I think there's room for a lot of improvement in the mechanism. The reason I would have helped Chrysler is not so much to prop up a major employer, although that's a valuable consideration. But a competitive analysis of the industry would have suggested that Chrysler was a viable competitor, for it has always been the least vertically integrated and, perhaps, the most technically innovative of the major American automobile companies.

Audience Member: Haven't our federal pollution-control standards hurt the auto and steel industries in regaining their competitive stature?

Kantrow: As far as the steel industry and pollution regulations are concerned, there are all kinds of ways to write air-quality standards. Some are stupid. Some make more sense. You can do what the EPA did at first and write them so that you must control every single point source of pollution in a steel plant, which is a phenomenally expensive way to do it. Or you can do it with something like a bubble policy, where there's one single emission standard for the whole plant, and you leave it up to the plant to figure out how to do it most efficiently. In the automobile industry, the corporate average fuel economy standards were announced in such a way that the automobile companies could meet them only by taking weight out of their cars. The auto companies looked at those standards and said,

"What we need is a quick and dirty solution; we do not have time for an elaborate technological fix. What will work in the time allowed is to make our cars lighter." That essentially was what they did. They pulled money out of research on alternate modes of propulsion.

Audience Member: You mentioned the contrast between the quality of Japanese products and those made in the United States. Would you comment on what influence, if any, collective bargaining may have had on the quality here in the United States?

Kantrow: I'm not sure the relevant term is "collective bargaining." I think the relevant term is "work rules." The Japanese labor situation often gets treated as being simpler and more homogeneous than it is. I would not want to trade American labor for Japanese. Yes, in a major sense they are nonunionized. They do have company unions, with top union leaders who have been managers, and vice versa. It's a different world.

What we see, and what I believe, is that there is a role for unions in American industry. Yet the union leadership, over the years, has been as responsible as management for the sorry fix we've gotten ourselves into. Employees could also get fat, happy, and sloppy, and management could buy them off with convenient work rules and a fatter paycheck.

The steel industry and the automobile industry were paying wages for years that were way out of line with the rest of the nation's labor force or any other rational standard. But they could afford to pay them because the industries were phenomenally profitable. They chose to buy labor peace rather than risk a strike.

The real issue is not so much the salary scale. It's not wages per hour; it's wages per hour actually worked. In 1979, it took Ford 112 hours to build a subcompact car; Toyo-Kogio, which manufactures Mazdas, took just 47. There's a difference in absolute wages rates, but there are many fewer labor hours. That's where the real kicker comes in. So wage rates are only part of it.

But the other part is this network of featherbedding work rules. If you've ever been in an American unionized plant when a line goes down, you know the characteristic posture adopted by the people at the machines. They stand at attention, waiting for the decision about which craft union to call.

Collective bargaining as a means to get those rules overturned offers hope. Collective bargaining has a place as a means to come to saner wage rate negotiations. I think the real villain here is the work rules, for which both sides are responsible. That's where they have to change.

ROSABETH MOSS KANTER

Providing the Corporate Environment to Foster Innovation

The innovation process describes what high-performance companies do well that can be incorporated into most American business enterprises. My goal is to help American companies gain a better understanding of what makes successful enterprises work.

That understanding would help us address what I call the "Roast Pig Problem," a perennial problem plaguing American management. I named this after a classic essay in nineteenth century British literature, "A Dissertation on Roast Pork," by Charles Lamb. Lamb wrote about the nature of knowing. In this particular essay, he gave us a parable about what happens when people do not fully understand what it takes to get the results they want.

In the essay, Lamb talked about an important innovation for the history of humanity, the discovery of cooking. He theorized that it took place ages ago, perhaps in ancient China, when people lived in primitive surroundings; animals wandered in and out of the houses, and people ate their food raw. One day, he imagined, a father left his oldest son to guard the house, and the son accidentally set the house on fire. When the father came back, he was poking through the ruins of the house to see if there was anything that could be salvaged. He happened to touch one of the neighborhood pigs that had been trapped in the house. Because the flesh was still warm, he put his fingers in his mouth to cool them off, and they tasted delicious. He had just discovered cooking. News of this spread in the village, and soon all the people in the neighborhood were burning their houses down.

The moral of the story is that if you don't understand why the pig gets cooked you're doomed to waste an awful lot of houses.

We've had a tendency to do that in American management. That's why I think this intellectual renaissance in business is just as exciting as the productivity renaissance. We're starting to figure out why things work, rather than mindlessly copying somebody else's system, rather than mindlessly implementing what they told us to do in business school. Rather, we now figure out exactly what it takes in each enterprise to get the results we need, given our products, our customers, and our markets. That same kind of understanding is important in addressing the innovation question.

How do we achieve sufficient levels of innovation without wasting the whole house in the process? Some experts today are advising companies that the way to get more innovation is to give lots of money to every man, woman, and child in the company to use to experiment. Toss many, many balls in the air, they advise, and you're sure to catch a few of them. The way to get more oil, they say, is just to drill more wells. The process can be more guided than that. You can get more productive innovation without spending all of our resources in the process.

There are clearly pressures for greater innovation today. A short list of some of the forces that I think are important would include the global economy, foreign competition, increased market competition in nearly every domestic market, and new technology. New technology is itself both an innovation and a source of pressure for more innovation to use it. Companies that incorporate new technology faster and more effectively have an advantage over those that do not. This is not automatic. Simply buying the equipment does not guarantee that it will be used appropriately.

There are also pressures because of political forces. We no longer dominate our sources of supply in this country or abroad; therefore, we have to be much more responsive to the actions of suppliers, including politically motivated groups that may decide to withhold critical raw materials, as OPEC decided to do with oil. Internally, both regulation and deregulation create the need for innovation. The health care industry is in turmoil today, partly because of government regulation and health care cost-containment legislation. At least four major business industries have been shaken up because of deregulation: airlines, trucking, telecommunications, and financial services. In all of these industries there are pressures for innovation in order to be competitive now that the rules of the game are changing.

And changes in people affect organizations, too. Demographic shifts in our population have changed the nature of consumer markets, as have new labor force attitudes inside organizations. These trends that started in the late 1960s and early 1970s are continuing and, in fact, changing shape. We have a more educated rights-conscious work force, looking not only for a voice in decisions, but also for a return on its human capital in the business. The entrepreneurship theme is being pushed not only by business leaders, but also by young business people who want a piece of the entrepreneurial action, even inside large corporations.

I summarize all those pressures in a tongue-in-cheek formula that says that "the MTBS is getting to be less than, or equal to, the MTMD." The MTBS is the "mean time between surprises." That time is getting shorter, regardless of the industry. We now have more surprises, or unplanned contingencies, whether they occur through the actions of foreign governments or our own government, through the actions of competitors, or through changes in technology. More surprises are controlled by more groups, and they are occurring at a more rapid rate.

When the surprise interval factor gets to be less than, or equal to, the MTMD factor, or "the mean time to make a decision," then the organization is in trouble. This is why the sluggish bureaucracy, the too-large, too-hierarchical organization that cannot make decisions quickly, is in trouble today for economic survival and success in this environment.

Innovation turns out to be critical for economic survival and success in this environment. Organizations must be able to innovate, anticipate, and react to surprises that could not have been planned for, no matter how good their planning mechanisms become. And they must have new responses ready, because the lead time for responses is shorter. Innovation is critical, because it is the way to solve problems. Innovation is the process of bringing new problem-solving or opportunity-addressing ideas into use.

Innovation is not the same thing as invention. In many cases, it is a question of using the things that have already been invented and making sure they are put to productive use. Not all innovation involves new products or new technology, nor is innovation confined to newer industries. The domain for innovation does change as products or services mature, because the rate of technological advance slows down. Products may eventually become commodities, or categories that are indistinguishable across producers and for which modifications mean little to the consumer. But the need for innovation does not disappear. It may just change domain, away from major product breakthroughs toward cost cutting or better packaging or better distribution.

Part of the planning task is to determine the key domains for innovation that fit the business life cycle. For example, one major consumer products company is putting a great deal of its innovation emphasis on manufacturing improvements, so that the company can restrain costs at a time when many of its products must compete against generic, or unbranded, products. Its innovations are in manufacturing, or in marketing, or in distribution, or sometimes in internal management systems—all domains for innovation that are important to older companies. Innovations in product and technology may be important to younger companies, but sometimes even they neglect other innovation domains, to their ultimate regret.

A computer company that is very innovative in product but which fails to innovate in manufacturing and marketing may suffer as it competes with an IBM that is more balanced in its innovation strategies. There is always a need for innovation in many areas.

In conducting the research for my book, *The Change Masters*, I looked at well over 115 innovations in major companies. I studied what it took to get them to happen and tried to find the environment that supported them. I looked beyond new products. I looked at innovations in productivity, innovations in quality, innovations in management systems. For instance, a new inventory tracking and reduction system saved General Electric large amounts of money. A divisionwide word processing system was an innovation for another company. Another was a new budget process that better integrated plant input and output dollars.

For some companies innovations in those domains are even more important than simple innovations in products. Thus, innovation is just as applicable to older industries as it is to new industries.

But innovations have greater requirements than simply carrying out routine managerial work or routine operations. They need more power tools in the form of information, resources, and support. To innovate in nearly any domain requires more information, and often that information is located outside the department that is pushing the innovation.

Innovations also tend to require extra money, sometimes even more than has been budgeted for research and development departments. I found that, when it came to truly innovative new products, even R&D groups often had to seek more money than had been budgeted. By definition, if innovations are things that have not been anticipated, it is difficult to know in advance what they will cost.

Finally, innovations require more support than carrying out routine operations, more meetings and presentations to sell the idea, more collaboration and teamwork to implement.

In short, to innovate is not easy or simple. It requires creating a context in which people can get easy access to the information, the resources, and the support they need to act on new ideas that solve problems.

The people who lead innovations I call "change masters." They have a special skill, just as do the organizations in which they flourish. They are adept at anticipating the need for productive change and leading it. Both aspects are important, because more good ideas are floating around in most organizations than anybody ever takes advantage of. There are good reports on the shelf; there are possible new product designs. The problem is not only thinking of the innovations, but also bringing them into being.

My research found that there were five essential things that change masters do to make things happen.

The first thing that change masters do is to use "kaleidoscope" thinking. The kaleidoscope is a device for seeing patterns. It takes a set of fragments and arranges them in a pattern. But when you twist it slightly or shake it up, those same fragments form an entirely different pattern. That's what an innovator is doing, looking at the same array of data, the same facts and figures that everybody else is seeing, but managing to get a new angle, or a new perspective, on them.

One company calls this upside-down thinking, in which the same facts and figures suddenly suggest another direction to take that would solve a problem by doing something new and different. That kind of thinking lies behind the discovery of many new products. One of my favorite examples is the invention of frozen vegetables by Clarence Birdseye, who had a produce business in the Northeast. But because he was an adventurer, and often moved outside of his produce business, he brought back a big idea from an unrelated context. On a trip to Labrador, he happened to see some fish caught in the ice, which the natives thawed later and ate. And he brought that idea back and invented frozen vegetables.

It is a sure bet that General Foods, owner of Birdseye, does not send its R&D people on expeditions to Labrador—but maybe they should. It would get them outside the context in which they are operating. Getting outside of one department, one unit, or one specialty seeds innovations because it permits new-angle thinking. The high-innovation companies all encourage people to get outside of their offices, outside of their departments, outside of their specialties.

"Management-by-walking-around" is such a buzz word at Hewlett-Packard because it does not just allow managers to get to know what their employees are thinking. It gets ideas exchanged across the boundaries that customarily limit and restrict thinking. Similarly, the 3M Company, famous for its never-kill-an-idea program, stages "idea fairs," in which people literally display their latest ideas; Standard Oil of Ohio (Sohio) holds interdepartmental ideas exchanges to get a clash of perspectives.

The second thing that the people who lead innovations have to do is to be able to provide a clear vision of the future and to explain why their company should be adopting a new idea, whether it is a productivity improvement or a new product. This step is absolutely critical, because any particular innovation is only positive in retrospect, after it has proved itself. Before that, it is risky and uncertain; it has to be sold to the skeptics, and people have to be instilled with faith that it can work.

In order to get anything new to happen, an organization must have people who will put themselves behind a new idea, stand up for it, and inspire other people to come with them, or it will never have change. That is why some organizations don't achieve much innovation—because nobody is willing to stand up and put themselves behind a new idea; at the first sign of opposition, they cave in.

This is what we call leadership. Great world leaders understand this. For example, when Martin Luther King led the march on Washington and said, "I have a dream," he didn't say, "I have a few ideas, there are some problems out there, maybe if somebody worked on it we'd change things." When Brigham Young led the Mormons to Utah, he said, "We're heading west." He didn't say, "We'll wander west for a while, but if it doesn't work we can always go to North Carolina." How many people would have agreed to go along?

The difference between success and failure at innovation often is a matter of time and persistence. Everything looks like a failure in the middle. At some point in the history of every successful product, every successful new system, it looked like a bust. That is why an economy that is based on quarterly stock prices will never get much innovation; the pressure is to pull out if you don't get a quick return.

Successful innovations benefit from vision and persistence. One consumer product now on supermarket shelves, making a lot of money for its company, was known as "Project Lazarus" in its development stage, because it had risen from the dead so many times. Four times, people in the company tried to kill it off, and four times, the development team argued successfully to save it.

The third thing an innovator must be able to do is to build a coalition of all the groups or individuals whose support is critical to making an idea work. We make a big mistake in American industry, sometimes, by assuming that single individuals with power can will innovations into being. Whether something succeeds or fails often is in the hands of many more people, including the sales force that has to sell it and the workers who have to manufacture it.

The people who lead innovations know how to draw together the sources of information, the sources of resources, and the sources of support that they are going to need to make ideas actually happen. They flourish in climates where they can cross boundaries and go right to whoever has the money, and the data, and pull to win support from the people who are going to be affected and have to implement the change.

In one computer company, this process of "buying in" is so well known that they have elaborated a whole language around the steps for finding the people whose backing will make an idea work. They say that buy-in starts with a process called "tin-cupping." Almost literally, they say, a manager is taking a tin cup in hand and walking around the organization to see who has some spare change to throw in, or some staff to lend, or a key report to contribute to the success of an idea. Through this process they get wider ownership. It does not become the plan only of Department X, so that Departments Y and Z are ready to kill it at the first signs of success. Those innovations shared more widely are the ones that are likely to succeed. In the process of tin-cupping, the manager gets back what the computer firm calls a "sanity check," a way to screen out bad ideas. This is a feedback process that does not permit the head of Department X to just march off in his or her own direction.

Fourth, the change masters who are effective at innovating are very good participative managers. They work through teams, because many innovations also fail in American companies because of inertia, or loss of momentum. Unless everyone involved feels fully committed, nothing will happen. So innovators do have to be good at building a sense of team spirit.

Finally, to bring it full circle, the innovation process requires another change master skill: ensuring that everyone involved feels they are going to be made a hero, sharing in the credit and recognition. For example, in one insurance company that does not particularly reward innovation, a regional manager raised productivity in his area dramatically. He increased profitability through a series of employee teams, all of which made modest improvements in their work areas. When bonus time came, upper management had decided to reward him with a big bonus. He went to them and asked for bonus money for the people below bonus-eligible who made this success possible. They said no. So he took $2,000 out of his own pocket and collected similar sums from the managers below him, and they created their own bonus pool that they gave to everyone who had contributed to the project down to the clerical workers. Not only was that part of the promise of getting people involved in productive change, but it also made it much more likely that they would enlist in the next change.

Getting more people engaged in innovation or creative problem solving often starts with middle-level people with a new idea, and this occurs much more readily in some kinds of environments than in others. There are a number of key characteristics that distinguish the high-innovation companies I examined from the innovation-stifling ones. They provided an environment that encouraged enterprise, that got people wanting to do more to raise quality, to raise levels of performance, to think of new ideas.

Jobs with broader scope, in which people have responsibility for results rather than following procedures manuals, encouraged enterprise. This factor encouraged people to reach beyond the definitions of how they have always done things toward whatever it would take to get the results they desire.

This idea violates conventional management wisdom, which for a long time preached the virtues of dividing jobs into as small units as possible, to get people to specialize and focus and to make distinctions between territories clear. That kind of thinking was ideal for a change-averse bureaucracy. But to inspire people to reach beyond current practice to make things better requires broader-scope jobs.

Thus, the new wave of progressive companies, including a major soap manufacturing company that is doing this on the shop floor, combine jobs rather than divide them up. In developing a joint factory venture with Toyota, General Motors has gotten the United Auto Workers to agree to combine jobs. Instead of having something like 20 to 25 job classifications in the plant, it will have only three. The plant will combine jobs so that people have a bigger sense of responsibility.

The structure of high-innovation companies also is different. They tend to be structured around much smaller units, each of which has autonomy. Thus, change masters can act. Approval is locally accessible, and there's a great deal of interdependence, or teamwork, across functions.

The smaller unit is where the whole team is represented, works together across any department and function, and can act—that is Hewlett-Packard's strategy and that is why HP is widely touted as one of the best managed companies in America. When divisions get to more than 2,000 people, or $100 million in sales, Hewlett-Packard breaks them into two divisions. Each will have a general manager who controls approval for local action, each will have profit responsibilities, and each will have the whole array of functions represented to work together interdependently. Smaller is getting to be more beautiful in American industry, even inside very large companies.

The next aspect of encouraging enterprise derives from the culture. High-innovation companies have what I call a "culture of pride" as opposed to a "culture of mediocrity or inferiority." They manage to send the message that all their people are potential "winners."

High-innovation companies select people carefully and promise them long-term employment. They spend more on training and development and career work. IBM perhaps spends more per employee on people-oriented management training than any other company in the country, and General Electric also ranks very high. These expenditures show the value of people.

Praise-abundance also marks high-innovation firms. The number of trophies, wall plaques, badges, celebrations, and parties that people achieve at Honeywell is astonishing. General Electric Medical Systems has what they call the "Attaboy" system of constant pats on the back or letters for the file. Of course, they make a point of recognizing people for outstanding achievement in more substantial ways.

This is not "soft" management. There also are a lot of standards to which people are held. But high-innovation companies make people feel that they *can* contribute. That's the exact opposite of what I saw in the low-innovation companies. One insurance company I studied turns to outsiders to make change. The attitude seems to be that "if you've worked here for more than two years, you must be a real turkey, because nobody here is capable of helping us change." They turn over the top executive group all the time. Six out of the nine top executives had less than two years with the company at the time I looked at them. They brought in new department heads from GE, or Citicorp, or IBM, every time they wanted change, as though they had no talent in the organization. They turned to consultants for every problem, even for trivia. Consultants should not be used to substitute for things that people inside could do. Literally, in that company, they hired a set of consultants to help them figure out how to speed up the efficiency of photocopying procedures manuals—something to which a team of people inside might have easily contributed.

Rewards are also in the high-innovation companies. They are more often *investment*-oriented than simply *payoff*-oriented. An investment is something one gets *before* one has achieved, in order to help him or her achieve, from which one might get a return; a payoff comes after the fact.

Classically, American industry has been quite bonus-and-awards–centered. But the high-innovation companies seem to be using a higher proportion of funds for before-the-fact investment. For example, 3M has an internal venture capital pool, and companies such as Eastman Kodak are setting up steering committees to fund employee proposals. For many entrepreneurial people, the biggest reward is the chance to do it in the first place, the chance to build a new department, the chance to lead a project team.

The second side of acting on one's ideas that high-innovation companies also provide is empowerment. These companies empower people to act on their ideas by making it easier for them to get the information, the support, and the resources they need—the three key power tools to make productive things happen.

Information is easier to get in high-innovation firms, because communication systems tend to be open rather than closed. The amount of operating data that is shared in the high-innovation companies is surprising even to insiders. But if they are expecting people to take responsibility to improve performance, then people need information. One company is using the personal computer effectively to make sure that data gets down to the lowest levels, so that people even at the bottom can innovate.

There are also policies in some of these companies against closed meetings; every meeting is open to anyone who wants to attend. The head of the CAT scanner business unit at General Electric Medical Systems observes that policy—a half-billion-dollar product line within one business unit of GE. It means that the information is there if people need it, when they want it.

Support is also easier to get in high-innovation companies. For one thing, there's more career mobility that takes people across fields and functions. They are much more likely to have unusual career moves in high-innovation companies, people jumping from finance to personnel to marketing.

They get people out and moving around the organization, the management-by-walking-around concept. One of the general managers I worked with at Honeywell has a goal for himself and each of his staff members that he puts on their annual management-by-objectives. It's called the "Take-a-Walk" goal: to be out there making contact, integrating, getting to know people, and therefore, becoming better able to collaborate because they are personally known.

Job security is important too. It lets people know that there's a future against which they can start to plan things that are longer term. Therefore, they are more likely to support each other's innovative ideas.

Innovative companies also are more likely to do more things in teams. They use many more task forces and project groups. They are less bound by hierarchy or by status. They pull people together, as needed, who have the skills to solve a problem. There is easier access up and down the hierarchy, across functions, across levels, and across departments.

The last thing that makes it possible for people to get the power to innovate is that resources are decentralized. More people control budgets and time. There are places to go if an innovator is turned down. Thus, more people can start experiments, because they can get the seed capital. At 3M, if a division manager turns down an idea, a person can go to the manager of another division, who also will have funds and might say yes.

This is all balanced by good planning, of course. High-performance companies get people working on the things that are important to the future of the organization. Because people know in what direction their company is headed, they can start contributing to it. The best-managed high-innovation companies also have the best planning systems and let that information be known to people at local levels, so they all can focus their activities in the same direction.

I define the high-innovation environment as integrative. People pull together, rather than pull apart. Territories overlap. Jobs have bigger scope. There is teamwork. People cross boundaries, move across functions, move out of their offices, and work together with a unity of purpose.

The kind of environment that stifles innovation is characterized by "segmentalism," in which each unit, each area, operates as though it were totally independent of the others, as if the others were the enemy. Segmentalism creates systemic roadblocks to innovation. When everyone's energy is taken up in guarding what they are doing from everyone else, a company does not get much innovation. Power tools are scarce in a segmentalist system, because information does not flow across those boundaries, people do not collaborate, and resources are doled out only from the top.

Segmentalist companies operate as though they do not want inno-vation at all, as though they observe a set of "rules for stifling innovation." The first such rule might be: Be suspicious of every new idea from below, because it is new, of course, and because it is from below; after all, if the idea were any good, we at the top would have thought of it already.

Second, insist that people who need your approval to act go through many other levels of the organization first. That way, you never have to say no. The idea probably will be killed off at a lower level.

Third, express criticism freely, withhold praise, and instill job inse-curity, because that keeps people on their toes. How else would they know you had standards? (This is the old macho school of management that says people do their best work when terrified. It's the opposite of the support and the security and the praise-abundance in higher inno-vation settings.)

Fourth, decide to change policies in secret and reorganize unexpect-edly, because that also keeps people on their toes. That avoids the anxiety, or the loss of productivity, that would occur if people knew in advance that change was coming. Better to let them learn on the radio as they are driving to work that the plant is closing. Under such con-ditions, people stop worrying about improving anything. They just do today's work, waiting for the next shoe to fall, and anyone who does have a development project can't do anything to help preserve it against the disruption of the change.

Fifth, be control-conscious. Count everything that can be counted, as often as possible. That way you insure that there are no spare paper clips, or spare dollars, or spare hours that could be directed into a project that wasn't planned at the top.

And, finally, never forget that you, at the top, already know everything important there is to know about the business. That way you don't have to be bothered by people who want to innovate.

In low-innovation companies, in short, change is seen as a threat and not as an opportunity. It is something to guard against. It is no wonder that I found such companies to be less successful on every financial measure.

To create and maintain a high-performance organization that is capable of innovating, to respond to the environment of more surprises requires hard work. It requires attention to the whole system and not just a special program to stimulate innovation or to raise productivity. This is a big commitment, but it is worth it.

Companies that are successful and want to keep on being successful do have to make the commitment to be innovative. In other words, if you want to keep on eating roast pork, you'd better go whole hog.

Audience Member: What is your opinion about the phrase "If you only knew what I know, you'd never disagree with me"?

Rosabeth Moss Kanter: You are saying there's some value to diversity, to having different viewpoints. I'm not sure we want organizations where everybody always agrees and they all know exactly what everybody else knows. That's why we have specialties and differences. There's more creative tension in the high-innovation settings. There is not automatic agreement, although I suppose if everybody did understand where everybody else was coming from, they would have a better understanding of their perspective. But, we want places where there's more diversity, more conflict and argument, because you get a better solution if it is argued out than if there's automatic agreement.

ROBERT P. FORRESTAL

Conference Summary

During the last two days, we have heard the stories of 11 high-performance companies. We heard from three relatively young companies, how they took root and how they grew in a sometimes hostile climate. We heard from four traditional companies, how they reorganized to survive and to compete more effectively while other mature firms were failing. We heard three leading southeastern banks describe their strategies for success in a deregulated environment. And we learned what others think of these companies. I'll review some of the main points.

MSA's Ken Millen explained why his company's philosophy of treating people as the key to success has opened the door for MSA to become the largest independent software supplier in the country. In his business, he said, the most important assets are good people who can develop and sell new software products and who can teach customers how to use them.

The Home Depot's Bernard Marcus taught us how his relatively new do-it-yourself lumber and hardware organization has achieved prompt recognition, partially because of the education provided to managers and employees.

Charter Medical Corporation's William A. Fickling, Jr., explained how companies can succeed by anticipating trends before anyone else does. Being first to meet a new demand, he said, can help a company be first to achieve profits from that trend.

The first speaker from a more traditional industry was Marvin Runyon of Nissan U.S.A., who described how he adapted his parent company's Japanese management strategies to his American operation. He attributed the success of his manufacturing facility to Nissan's principles of teamwork, to its lean corporate structure with relatively few layers of management, and to its emphasis on quality.

C. Martin Wood III of Flowers Industries detailed how to use the decentralized approach to management most effectively by giving responsibility to the workers closest to the decisions.

John Savage of Nucor Corporation emphasized the growth and success that companies can enjoy by motivating employees through programs such as profit sharing.

Mark C. Hollis expounded on Savage's theme by showing us how employees at Publix Super Markets have been motivated by stock ownership. All of Publix's stock is owned by employees, and 35 percent of Publix's pretax earnings are paid directly to employees in bonuses and pensions.

The first banker we heard from was Joel Wells of Sun Banks of Florida, who detailed how to get feedback from both employees and customers and how to implement suggestions.

Robert Strickland of Trust Company of Georgia, one of the most profitable banks in the Southeast, reminded us that companies not only need to establish programs to encourage excellence, but must maintain and sustain them. He said Trust Company's heritage is an important asset for today's management to maintain.

Thomas H. Jacobsen of Barnett Banks of Florida, the largest banking organization in the Sixth Federal Reserve District, briefed us on his bank's entrepreneurial spirit that encourages innovations through experimentation.

Rounding out the perspective from the financial services industry was Gerald Eickhoff of Bank Earnings International. He told us how his company leverages a consulting operation that makes money by helping banks become more efficient.

M. Kathryn Eickhoff of Townsend-Greenspan gave us an economist's viewpoint on the importance of profits. She said economic growth depends on investments that, in turn, depend on corporate profits. She made us more aware of the importance of recognizing high-performance companies.

The Federal Reserve's Preston Martin, who has watched corporations from both sides of the regulatory fence, emphasized the importance of three critical factors: innovation, productivity, and economic policy. Then we heard a Wall Street perspective from Eugene Epstein, who also conveyed the importance of corporate innovation for national economic growth.

We also heard from two authors specializing in management. Rosabeth Moss Kanter said we need to provide the corporate environment to foster innovation; she warned that only those companies that embrace change will have a chance to compete beyond the 1980s. Alan M. Kantrow described the way management can be the key to the industrial renaissance of our nation's traditional industries.

We thank each speaker for sharing these success stories with us. Though the companies represented at this conference are widely different, they share much in common. We learned, for instance, that each has remained at the forefront of change, consistently utilizing the most modern tools available in its industry. Each has found its niche in the market, and— critically important—each has developed strong empolyee-management relationships to build a team spirit into its organization.

We need now to think about what each has shared with us, then to incorporate what may be applicable into our own organizations. If our companies can compete more effectively in our region and around the world, perhaps in the future we'll be able to avoid the shortcomings that have plagued our nation's industrial machine in the recent past. Judging from what we have heard at this conference, we must remember always that real results come from innovation, entrepreneurship, productivity— and a recognition that any management can accomplish those goals best by working in harmony with the men and women in its offices and in its factories.

Appendix

High-Performance Companies in the Southeast: What Can They Teach Us?

American business is seeking fresh initiatives to overcome the economic inertia of the past decade. Poor productivity gains, decaying mature industries, and prolonged high unemployment have defied traditional solutions. Bold initiatives seem necessary to launch the American economy on a new course of extended prosperity. Rather than study economic solutions grounded in foreign cultures, with different political and social values that contribute to the effectiveness of such measures, the Federal Reserve Bank of Atlanta has examined models of success closer to home—in the southeastern United States.

This study concentrates on corporate growth models to reappraise the basic American business climate. Some scholars see the entrepreneur, the calculated risk-taker, as the hero in the saga of economic growth. Research that focuses on the management side of entrepeneurship, therefore, may be a useful way of refocusing on incentive systems at the microeconomic level. We looked at 22 high-performance southeastern companies to learn whether common patterns underlie their outstanding profitability and growth rates (see box on "How Companies Were Selected"). Identifying characteristics shared by high-performance companies of strikingly different size and output, from small high-technology businesses to mature firms producing familiar commodities, could help renew the entrepreneurial spirit that established the United States as the unrivaled land of opportunity.

This six-month project (see box on "The Case Study Approach")

developed from a 1983 study of high-technology firms carried out by the Atlanta Fed.[1] Researchers in that study were struck by the link between the growth of high-tech firms and their application of modern management principles. They suggested investigating whether similar practices prevailed at rapidly growing companies in other industries. We did, in fact, find such patterns, which this article will describe in detail. These patterns are (1) a major emphasis on innovation, particularly in the area of technology; (2) an entrepreneurial management style that keeps organizational structures lean and flexible for prompt action and willing to take risks that promise high returns; (3) a view of employees as associates or affiliates— the company's most valued long-term asset—rather than as adversaries; and (4) an ongoing attention to marketing strategy that sharply defines the company's comparative advantages.

Outstanding southeastern companies adhere to a number of common management principles, judging from this major Atlanta Fed study. These shared principles might help revive America's productivity.

All four traits are grounded in corporate culture or identity, which makes the company—for consumers, employees, and management—more than the sum of the products and profits it produces. This identity or mission expresses the nature of such firms as social institutions, generating a dynamic community spirit similar to that of a pioneer community of the past or a winning athletic team of the present. We developed the acronym **Team** to refer to the key patterns we found—technology, entrepreneurship, affiliation, and marketing—all embedded in a common spirit or culture (see box on "Modern Management Theory"). We believe the "winning teams" we have studied offer valuable lessons for the renewal of the American free-enterprise system. The hero, the entrepreneur, the calculated risk-taker, are basic ingredients of the American dream. As models they are standards for innovation, creativity and excellence.

MAJOR FINDINGS

Technology/Innovation

We found that the companies we interviewed are engaged in some form of change or innovation. Many are pioneering products and processes never used before. Innovative activity often permeates the organization. Many firms innovate by applying experience from other industries or by deviating from tradition. Innovation frequently takes the form of technological change. Technology is applied with a sensitivity to all concerned—employees using equipment, customers enjoying the results, and shareholders realizing improved earnings.

Innovation and applications of technology are related to other characteristics we found in high-performance companies. Accepting change fosters an entrepreneurial bias toward action in management. Technology is often required in order to act quickly in a changing environment. Human resource management is enhanced by technology. Dirty and unpleasant jobs may be eliminated. In some cases, people are given greater responsibility and training for higher skilled jobs. High-performance companies tend to retrain and reassign workers who are displaced by technology. These companies' fast growth plus the care and feeding of technically advanced machinery usually provide jobs for employees.

Market strategy is also tied closely to innovation and technology. Many successful companies view technology as a competitive weapon. They are constantly looking for more efficient ways to do things. These companies are typically market leaders in some aspect of their business. They believe that to remain ahead of the competition they have to be on the forefront of change. If they are constantly playing catch-up in technology, they are constantly playing catch-up in the marketplace. The companies we interviewed embrace change by using state-of-the-art technology, redefining their target market, offering new delivery systems, or introducing innovative products.

State-of-the-Art Technology in Mature Industries. Some companies have found that, in order to compete in commodity businesses and against foreign producers with relatively low labor costs, they must adopt advanced technology.[2] Automation of the production process is almost an obsession with some of the companies we studied. Keeping up with technology is a continuous process that requires shopping widely for existing technology, helping suppliers design more functional equipment, finding ways to make equipment more flexible through computerization techniques, and evaluating new equipment. Technology used in production processes at many of the companies we visited was developed by foreign firms.

Manufacturers in commodity businesses can no longer rely on lower wage southern labor to man their factories. To excel as low-cost producers, they believe they must automate. Four companies we interviewed stood out in this respect: Nissan U.S.A., Russell Corporation, Nucor Corporation, and Flowers Indusries. (Although not a manufacturer competing with low-cost foreign producers, Delta Air Lines also scored high in our sample as a leader in technology. Delta keeps its fleet equipped with the most modern airliners flying.) Nissan, a Smyrna, Tennessee subsidiary of the Japanese car and truck producer, had the opportunity to fully automate its facility, constructed in the early 1980s. The company has almost 230 robots in use, handling unpleasant and dangerous jobs such as painting and welding. They can be programmed to adjust automatically to different size and model vehicles, thereby allowing a more flexible production schedule. Russell Corporation, an Alexander City, Alabama textile and apparel manufacturer specializing in athletic clothing, operates one of the most automated textile manufacturing facilities in the Southeast. Gene Gwaltney, the firm's chief executive

Modern Management Theory

In the past several years, popular interest in management has reached a new peak. Books on the subject have topped the best-seller list for months. Our economic malaise has contributed to widespread interest in management as cause and cure for such problems as lagging productivity and slow economic growth. We used these works as a reference point as we interviewed financially successful companies in the Southeast, although we attempted to remain receptive to new principles.

One book that influenced our initial thinking was **In Search of Excellence**. The authors, Thomas J. Peters and Robert Waterman Jr., identify eight management principles employed by large American corporations that had survived over decades of good and bad economic conditions. These eight include (1) the conscious propagation of a company's values or mission among all employees through credos, rituals, and myths; (2) achievement of high productivity through concerned attention to employees; (3) lean management structure that fends off bureaucratic tendencies, such as long memos, committees, and complex procedures commonly found in large, established organizations; (4) an atmosphere of procedural informality akin to that found at smaller companies ("loose/tight" principles); (5) close attention to customers; (6) a bias toward action (rather than forming committees or studying proposals too long); (7) product continuity (rather than conglomerate-style diversification); and (8) a spirit of entrepreneurship and autonomy that fosters product development and decision-making at the lowest levels. By fostering these eight principles of management, Waterman and Peters assert, large, mature companies can retain many desirable traits of smaller firms.

Another book that addressed these questions is Rosabeth Moss Kanter's **The Change Masters: Innovation for Productivity in the American Corporation**. We sought to determine whether the innovation-fostering traits identified by Kanter were present at the companies we interviewed. These traits include a pervasive spirit of autonomy and an atmosphere of brisk intellectual interchange that keep these companies from becoming complacent and that force them to be aware of their changing environment and the need to adapt with it.

A recent study commissioned by the American Business Conference to identify characteristics common to successful mid-sized companies reiterated patterns described by Waterman and Peters.* One important

addition with regard to these smaller companies was market orientation. Mid-sized growth companies tend to produce for a well-defined niche, and they fit into that niche not as the low-cost producer but as suppliers of a high value-added product or service that bespeaks quality and commands a higher price and profit.

Our focus on individual companies as the catalyst of economic development led us to look for signs of an entrepreneurial management style: "Entreprenuers," as one researcher summed up, "are responsible for a significant amount of the change in our society, much of the economic growth, practically all of the sustained growth in employment, plus the new technologies that make our life easier and more enjoyable and the new drugs and medical instruments that keep us healthy and cure us when we are sick."**

Finally, we acknowledge our debt to a variety of works (see bibliography), such as **The Art of Japanese Management, Theory Z**, and to research by George Odiorne, Peter Drucker, and others on modern principles of management. Those works extol a participative and collegial rather than hierarchical, authoritarian style of leadership, cooperative rather than adversarial employee relations, and management respect for the contribution of employees to the company's success.

We organized traits cited as important in the literature into four areas. These areas are, with one exception, those defined in classical economics as the factors of production—land, labor, capital, and entrepreneurship. We looked at companies' products and how they are marketed, their treatment of labor, utilization of capital (both human and physical capital and the attendant role of technology), and management or entrepreneurship. We gave little attention to land, or possession of special resources such as oil deposits or patents, because we were seeking aspects of management with more universal application. We do not deny their importance. Indeed, officials of the Coca-Cola Company assert that their trademark is one of the most critical factors in the corporation's long-lived success.

Within the remaining areas—product, management, employees, and capital, we sought to determine whether management principles frequently cited in recent works prevailed at high performing southeastern companies. Not surprisingly, we found some successful companies that defied several of these management principles. Nonetheless, our research indicates that these principles seem generally applicable to financially successful companies based in the Southeast.

---

*The Winning Performance of Mid-sized Growth Companies," American Business Conference (May 1983).

Silver, David A. **The Entrepreneurial Life, New York: John Wiley & Sons, 1983), p. 1.

officer, goes so far as to say, "If you wait until you can cost justify a piece of equipment, you're too late. You can't afford not to have the latest technology in place."

Nucor, a Charlotte, N.C. steel manufacturer, uses continuous casting, a technologically advanced process used extensively in Europe and Japan, to produce steel. Nucor managers continue to seek the latest technologies by traveling abroad to learn about research, development and utilization. Flowers Industries, a Thomasville, Georgia baked goods company, succeeds where others have failed by buying near-bankrupt bakeries, modernizing the plant and equipment, and achieving economies of scale through reciprocal baking.

Adding Noncommodity Lines of Business in Mature Industries. Some of the more mature companies find it wise to seek higher value-added products and diminish their dependence on traditional commodity lines of business. Diversifying out of mass production of low-priced standard goods during the last several years helped two southeastern companies, Sonoco Products, a South Carolina-based paper products company, and Oxford Industries, an apparel firm based in Atlanta, outperform their peers in declining industries. While the products were familiar to the American consumer, the transition into value-added businesses was a radical departure from these companies' historical experience. By seeking products with higher margins and a market niche, these two companies transformed themselves into value-added producers, and their orientation shifted from production to marketing.

From its inception, Sonoco Products has been tied closely to the textile industry because it produces paper and plastic cones onto which thread or yarn is wound. Sonoco's leaders redefined their business as industrial packaging, which enabled them to move into other items, such as paper cans used for packaging orange juice, potato chips, and motor oil. Oxford Industries was a private-label apparel producer until its top management realized that it was unprofitable to compete with lower-cost, foreign producers. To establish a greater perceived value for its goods, it took advantage of the designer trend in clothing. The company has exclusive production rights to the Ralph Lauren Polo line of boys clothing and has added other designer labels. Days Inn, another Atlanta-based firm we interviewed, is in a low-price commodity business—renting economy

rooms to cost-conscious travelers. Richard Kessler, CEO, has sought to add value to those rooms by stressing high quality, friendly service, consistent products, and good hotel design.

Offering New Delivery Systems in an Old Business. Several companies we interviewed were innovative in designing a new way to deliver an old product or service. Federal Express, a Memphis-based delivery service, uses computerized dispatching rather than the traditional radio dispatching. This system enables the firm to improve the efficiency of its delivery system. Home Depot, an Atlanta-based retailer, found it could reduce costs and prices by eliminating the warehouse link in the distribution chain of the lumber and home-repair retail industry. Its retail stores function as the warehouses. The firm's discount prices, variety of goods, and well-trained sales assistants have produced rapid growth for the relatively new company. Key Pharmaceutical, a Miami-based drug manufacturer, boasts an innovative delivery system involving new technologies in delivering proven drugs to the patient's system. One of the company's lead products, Nitro-Dur, continuously administers the proper dose of nitroglycerin to a heart patient by means of a patch worn against the skin. The drug is "delivered" to the body through the skin rather than through the mouth.

Wachovia Bank and Trust Company, headquartered in Winston-Salem, N.C., pioneered a new delivery system for banking services in the early 1970s. It assigned a "personal banker" to every retail customer who has an account at one of its branches. The personal banker coordinates the customer's deposit and loan accounts and any other financial service needs. To accomplish this one-on-one attention, Wachovia had to establish a computerized means of assimilating and dispensing demographic and account information about each customer.

Offering a Product Previously Unavailable. Product innovation at high-performance companies takes place continuously to supplement or replace old products reaching their maturity. However, two companies applied existing technology in new situations to serve a previously unmet market need. Publix Super Markets, based in Lakeland, surprised the Florida banking system when it announced the introduction of its own automated teller machine (ATM) network in which banks could participate. The supermarket chain is one of the first in the country to place multibank ATMs in every store. It also jumped the gun on banks by establishing its own computerized point-of-sale payment system.

Federal Express' initial product was so unique that it started a new industry. The Memphis company popularized the small-package air express business in the early 1970s and remains the market leader. Today Federal Express is expanding its boundaries with its new Gemini project, which will transmit facsimiles of documents by satellite rather than by airplane.

We did find notable exceptions to the general rule of companies being on the cutting edge of innovation and technology. For example, Coca-Cola officials place much more value on the proper timing of innovation. They purposely wait until the first generation of a new product or technique has proven its viability and revealed its flaws. Then Coke, capitalizing upon the mistakes of its predecessors, moves in, seeking to dominate the market. Officers of the Atlanta-based Trust Company bank holding organization also stated their preference to follow in the footsteps of technological leaders and innovators.

Balance. Perhaps more important than the cautiousness implicit in this attitude toward technology is the widespread sense of balance we found. Many officials indicated the need to apply technology without losing the human touch. The companies we visited displayed a sensitivity to humanizing the workplace despite the high degree of automation surrounding workers. Assembly line workers at Nissan, for instance, had been allowed to place potted plants and hanging baskets in their work areas.

Many companies emphasized that, although a particular service or procedure theoretically can be performed more efficiently by a machine than by a person, a people-oriented approach makes more sense. Federal Express uses a surprisingly manual process to sort packages. "We have considered every possible technology to automate this process," one officer told us. "We have rejected most suggestions because they inconvenience the customer or they cost more than the labor-intensive process that we currently use."

Pervasive Innovation. We found companies where innovation is a way of life. It is evident not only in high-level decision making but also in the way the line workers do their jobs and middle managers seek to improve operations. Production workers at Key Pharmaceuticals often suggest

ways to improve the equipment to make the output more efficient. They know that Key is growing fast enough to redistribute workers, so they readily suggest improvements to reduce the number of workers on a line. Plant managers at Flowers Industries are responsible for requesting new equipment for their bakeries. Each middle manager researches available equipment and decides what is best for his operation. When we visited Flowers, a supervisor had obviously rigged a piece of equipment to keep the bread straight on the conveyor. It was his responsibility to get a high-quality product out the door on time, so he took the initiative to improve the operation.

In most cases, innovation is more prevalent, or more apparent, at higher-level decision-making posts. We found little evidence of new product development at the grass roots that Waterman and Peters described. Fred Smith, chief executive of Federal Express, commented that he does not want innovation everywhere in the company. Certain guidelines must be followed, he says; deviations may cause problems further down the line. Workers are not free to change these standards at will. Yet, we found that workers often suggest changes that are reviewed by industrial engineers to see how they fit into the whole process.

When new processes are being developed, those who will eventually be doing the work are consulted to help optimize the procedure. Nissan's industrial engineers consult assembly workers, who often suggest better ways to do a job. Russell operators and maintenance technicians help evaluate new equipment. Publix's store managers and clerks work with the technical staff in designing and implementing customer-related computer systems.

Technology Transfer. We found that much innovation occurs by technology transfer, taking a concept or process from one industry and applying it to another. Publix applied banking technology (ATMs and point-of-sale terminals) to its supermarket business to reduce losses from bad checks and processing costs. Key Pharmaceuticals adapted food production methods and explosives technology to its production of nitroglycerin drug patches. On the product side, unlike pharmaceutical companies that refuse to promote products not invented by their own researchers, Key looks outside the company for new technology it can turn into profitable products. Charter Medical of Macon, Georgia applied expertise from real estate to the health care industry; for Charter, a hospital management company specializing in psychiatric care, the result is a system that emphasizes patient satisfaction and returns a profit largely by cost reduction. Bank Earnings, Inc. has combined technology in the banking industry with their own marketing program, by applying microcomputers to the solution of operations problems at commercial banks.

Much of the technology transfer occurs because officers of the company have experience in other industries. This often facilitates the cross-pollination of ideas. One top manager at Key Pharmaceuticals had worked previously for Ford Motor Company. Federal Express's top officers bring experience from the airline, travel, and computer industries. Nucor's CEO is an aeronautical engineer by training with long experience in metallurgy but none in the steel industry prior to taking over Nucor.

Entrepreneurial Management

An important factor in the success of companies we studied was their entrepreneurial management style—the "E" of our "TEAM" principles. We found management to be lean, informal, and action-oriented. However, we found other patterns that ran counter to expectations derived from recent books (see box on "Modern Management Theory"). We had anticipated a participative management style, characterized by decentralization, autonomy, and an atmosphere of spirited but friendly dissent. We found two distinct styles, one centralized, the other decentralized. At many companies, CEOs and their top colleagues told us that they are personally involved in operations, organization is fairly centralized, and that cohesiveness, especially among the top management team, is much more characteristic than dissent. At others, decentralization prevailed, with considerable low-level autonomy and lively debate.

High-performance companies instill a sense of ownership, an action-oriented entrepreneurial spirit throughout their organization. They do so not only through financial incentives but, more importantly, through the definition and communication of a corporate mission. Almost none of the companies we visited based management primarily on efficiency, financial returns or other quantitative norms. While such standards are important, they consider vision, corporate culture, and other qualitative norms equally significant, especially in the company's long-run success.

Identity. Virtually all the companies we visited had a keen sense of identity. This identity determines the norms by which a firm chooses products to market, implements technology, treats employees, and generally organizes and manages its affairs. A self-conscious view of one's company as a social institution embodying far more than financial values was widespread and strong among our sample.

Dennis Hayes, CEO and founder of Hayes Microcomputer Products in Atlanta, says he grew frustrated with the bureaucratic malaise at two large companies where he worked. He says he decided to leave the security of a corporate engineering job to "build the great American company." He wanted to create a place where people would want to come to work, would be committed to and enthusiastic about their jobs and would be able to achieve more of their human potential.

Many companies expressed their identity through a formal statement of philosophy. Nowhere was this more evident than at Nissan. Marvin Runyon, the CEO, has evolved this statement of purpose: "To build the best quality trucks sold in North America." The slogan is posted in the plant for all employees to see, remember, and strive for.

Publix, on the other hand, defines itself as the company where "shopping is a pleasure." Publix workers hold this as their primary goal. Federal Express's stated mission is to solve people's high-priority logistics problems. "People-service-profit" is a shorthand version of this mission that is transmitted to all employees. Charter Medical's purpose is "to provide quality health care through the free enterprise system." Sun Banks, a Florida bank holding company based in Orlando, also has a formal mission statement. Its essence is that Sun Banks' purpose is to please, not just satisfy, customers, employees, and shareholders. Days Inn is formulating a statement about the high quality of lodgings it offers and the attendant high value to its customers. This statement will be displayed in all its motel lobbies. CEO Richard Kessler already stresses the importance of inculcating employees with the company "mindset" so he can turn over more responsibility to them.

No formal credo exists at other companies we visited, but a link between the product marketed and the company's identity is strong. Coca-Cola President Donald Keough told us that Coke is more than a product; it's a moment of pleasure, a set of life experiences as reflected in customer collections of Coke memorabilia. This special experience that surrounds the product is felt not just by customers but also by Coca-Cola's 40,000 employees. Sam Ayoub, Coke's chief financial officer, mentioned the old saying that "Coke, not blood, runs through the veins of employees," implying that the staff is involved in the spirit of the company. Some high-performance firms elicit special loyalty from employees and customers because of their role as social institutions. Both Trust Company and Coca-Cola have contributed to the historical development of Atlanta. Sun Banks also sees community development in all the areas where it operates as an important aspect of its corporate identity.

Symbols serve as surrogates or reinforcement for formal credos. Tenure pins are common. Upon joining Management Science America (MSA), an Atlanta-based software developer, each employee receives a Tiffany-designed silver key. After five years this is replaced with a gold pin. Coke has pins for different tenure, including a diamond pin for 25 years service. Ties carrying the company logo are also to be found at such firms as Trust Company and Sun Banks. Federal Express and Coke operate company stores with an assortment of products carrying the company logo. At Federal these range from T-shirts to luggage. Uniforms are another way of fostering company identity. Nissan issues all employees slacks, T-shirt, shirt, and jacket. Wearing the uniform is voluntary. The plant is a heterogeneous mixture, with some employees wearing only their own clothes, others wearing the Nissan jacket over personal attire, and some sporting the Nissan T-shirt. Days Inn issues its front desk employees well styled and tailored uniforms. Thus, self-pride is integrated with pride in one's company. Quadram Corporation, a subsidiary of the Atlanta-based Intelligent Systems Corporation, a manufacturer of computer peripherals and graphics, created a new trademark—"Quadram Quality," or QQ—but management told employees it could not be displayed until the return rate on all products was reduced to less than one-half of one percent. Today, with that goal long since achieved, the symbol is entrenched in the Georgia microcomputer firm's corporate identity.

Finally, design and architecture reflect the company's identity. At Trust Company's headquarters in downtown Atlanta, three pillars from the former building that stood for half a century have been preserved near the entrance. A portion of the old facade is incorporated into an interior wall in the lobby. These architectural touches reinforce Trust Company's sense of history. Officials of the bank today speak of a strong sense of stewardship toward their legacy. Trust Company prides itself on sound financial practices, conservatism, and quality.

Credos and symbols are not typical of all the companies we visited. Nucor eschews such trappings as tenure pins. It recognizes length of service by giving employees shares of stock. However, such recognition is quite in keeping with the company's no-nonsense view of itself and its industry. CEO Ken Iverson told us: "Steel-making is hot, noisy, dangerous, dirty work, and there's no getting around that." In this environment, he believes, fancy ties and tenure pins would be totally inappropriate.

Two-Way Communications. Besides communicating the corporate mission and values, high-performance companies emphasize communications in general. What makes the emphasis on communications at these companies special is that it is two-way and linked with a willingness to respond to complaints, problems, or suggestions. Many update employees regularly about the companies' financial performance. Flowers' management emphasizes to employees that the best security for keeping their jobs and assuring advancement opportunity is through profit. They give employees an opportunity to share in those results. Nucor and Sonoco also stress the importance of informing employees about the company's fortunes. Fred Smith of Federal Express says, "For people to have pride in what they are doing, they must be constantly informed about the importance of their jobs and the results they are attaining."

Communications take many forms. Sun Banks and Sonoco keep their employees informed through newsletters and videotapes. Daily newsletters, containing information about new policies, pricing, products, recent performance, problems, and even personal stories, are read to station and hub employees at Federal Express.

Meetings are a widespread means of two-way communications. Nucor's general managers and often the CEO meet once or twice a quarter with groups of 50 employees to discuss business conditions. Sun Banks CEO Joel Wells visited all his company's banks to encourage bank presidents to do the same regularly. MSA's CEO, John Imlay, and its chief operating officer, Bill Graves, meet personally with all employees once or twice a year. Such meetings serve not only to keep corporate staff knowledgeable about line operations; they also provide a means for employees to become informed about the company, to voice suggestions, and to seek action on grievances. At Nissan, groups of 20 employees have lunch with CEO Marvin Runyon. These meetings have apparently won a reputation for trouble-shooting; once the ice ·is broken, employees bring out lists of complaints and problems. When we interviewed him, he apologized for being late, saying he had to call a manager to convey a suggestion an assembly line worker had made during lunch.

At Sonoco, 36 workers are chosen at random to have lunch with CEO Charles Coker once a month. In addition, Sonoco has an advisory board consisting of 10 elected employee representatives and 10 appointed managers. Flowers sends teams from headquarters every 18 months to interview groups of production line employees; the latter, guaranteed anonymity, air concerns and grievances, and suggest changes in management policies and practices Days Inn's top officers meet quarterly with employee peer groups, such as chambermaid supervisors, to inform them of the company's current financial condition and discuss problems. High-performance companies stress that bottom-up communication works only when management acts on the suggestion or explains why nothing can or should be done about the problem.

Personal Involvement. The emphasis on two-way communications is closely related to another aspect of entrepreneurial management—personal involvement of senior management in the company operations, a top-level attention to detail that results in lean organization and a minimum of bureaucratic formality. Days Inn's Richard Kessler, who typifies that personal involvement, insists on being informed of all decisions. He spends a day each month with the company's top 20 managers just below the senior staff; the meetings keep him abreast of potential problems and "bad news" he might not hear from senior officers. Kessler says that he does at times delegate authority; however, he believes that

Days Inn's growth requires intense involvement on his part. Charles Muench, chairman of Intelligent Systems, on the other hand, is the archetypal entrepreneur. He likes to invent new products and to get new companies off the ground. Once the company is on its feet, he likes to turn over routine management problems to someone else.

This type of personal involvement reinforces high-performance companies' mission and entrepreneurial spirit through the personalities of the CEO. A senior officer at Federal Express told us, "It's hard to overestimate the influence of Fred Smith." His energy and vision clearly mold the company and influence its every action. Most CEOs, however, exert influence through their ideas more than the sheer strength of their personality. Bernard Marcus of Home Depot personifies the enthusiastic, energetic sales-oriented personality that he hopes company employees bring to their jobs. He told visitors he was taking on a short tour of corporate headquarters, "You'll have to walk faster than that. Hurry up, this is retail!"

Personal involvement is not limited to CEOs. Many companies have work-sharing programs designed to keep corporate leaders in touch with the company's basic operations. For example, Sun Banks' senior management spends one and one-half days a quarter first relearning a basic function such as customer service, credit approval, or data processing, and then actually performing such activities in a local bank. Federal Express sends teams composed of one senior officer and his staff to work at the firm's Memphis hub, where packages are sorted and routed to final destinations. This is intense work at breakneck speed, conducted between midnight and 4 a.m. Such "hub blitzes," as they are called, help keep corporate headquarters in touch with the core of Federal's operations.

Several companies have "apprenticeship" programs for entry-level managers, particularly those whose specialties, such as law and accounting, will tend to remove them from line operations. Flowers requires incoming lawyers and financial analysts to get a feel for the business by working temporarily in the bakeries or as route salesmen driving delivery trucks. Home Depot put a rising company lawyer on the sales floor for several months to give him a better perspective. Management trainees at Oxford must make a garment, using every piece of machinery in the plant. At Publix all management personnel must begin by

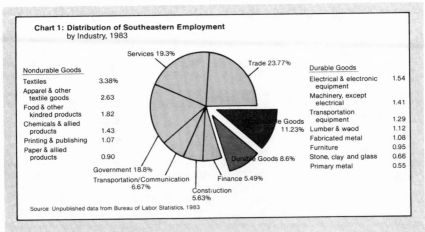

Chart 1: Distribution of Southeastern Employment
by Industry, 1983

Services 19.3%

Trade 23.77%

Nondurable Goods

Textiles	3.38%
Apparel & other textile goods	2.63
Food & other kindred products	1.82
Chemicals & allied products	1.43
Printing & publishing	1.07
Paper & allied products	0.90

e Goods 11.23%

Durable Goods 8.6%

Durable Goods

Electrical & electronic equipment	1.54
Machinery, except electrical	1.41
Transportation equipment	1.29
Lumber & wood	1.12
Fabricated metal	1.08
Furniture	0.95
Stone, clay and glass	0.66
Primary metal	0.55

Government 18.8%

Transportation/Communication 6.67%

Finance 5.49%

Construction 5.63%

Source: Unpublished data from Bureau of Labor Statistics, 1983

How Companies Were Selected

Our pool of 22 high-performance southeastern companies came from discussions with regional securities analysts, from formal nominations by the 44 directors of the Federal Reserve Bank of Atlanta and its five branches, and our own reading of current business literature. We used this screening method initially to ensure that we drew on the opinions of respected business leaders and financial analysts in selecting exceptional, privately held companies as well as publicly traded corporations.

We asked for nominations from the Atlanta Fed's directors because of their business backgrounds and their geographic diversity. Directors are respected business people and community leaders. Geographic representation is evenly dispersed throughout the District.[1] We asked each director to name three firms headquartered in the Southeast that he or she personally endorsed as being well-managed and likely to sustain their current success. Directors were asked to limit their selections to companies, public or private, large enough to have some impact on the local economy—preferably over $10 million in sales.

Nominated companies were subjected to a quantitative financial screen using industry data obtained from Standard and Poors (S&P). Our screen compared current and historical performance measurements for individual companies with those for their industry. Nominated companies passed this screen if they out-performed their industry peers. Our two measurements of current profitability were return on assets and return on equity for 1982. These ratios measure a firm's efficient use of its assets and its return to shareholders. We also were interested in summarizing each company's

historical performance and thus selected the five-year compound growth rate of net sales to measure its performance over time. Net sales measure the growth of a company more clearly than net income because a dramatic change in sales volume requires operational adjustment over time.

We compared each nominated company's measures of current and historical performance with those of its peer group—which we defined as companies headquartered in the Southeast with the same three or four-digit Standard Industry Classification (SIC). Each company measurement within an industry peer group was compared to the S&P national industry average for that same measure. Nominated companies were accepted into the pool of high-performance companies if their 1982 profitability and sales growth figures exceeded their industry average. We made this comparison to assure that each company stood out among its southeastern as well as its national peers. Companies selected were, in all cases, among the top in their peer group.[2]

Banks were subjected to different financial tests. Because of the sensitivity of the Fed's position as an industry regulator, we analyzed banks from a stockholder's point of view rather than from a regulatory standpoint. Banks were screened on four quantitative measurements: current price-earnings ratio, net interest margin, return on assets and five-year compound growth rate of total assets. These assessed each institution's current and historical performance relative to its southeastern peer group. For convenience, we limited our selection of banks to the ten largest in the region, although we recognize that many small banks are well-managed and highly profitable.

138   Appendix

Table 1. Bank Performance Rankings
     (1 = highest)

Ranked by Total Assets September 30, 1983	Price-Earnings Ratio	1982 Net Interest Margin	1982 Return on Average Assets	5-Year Compound Growth Rate of Total Assets
NCNB	10	9	7	3
Barnett Banks of Florida	5	2	4	2
Sun Banks	4	4	6	4
Southeast Bank	8	7	8	7
Wachovia	3	8	2	9
C&S	6	6	5	10
First Union	7	8	10	1
First Atlanta	9	5	3	8
Trust Company	1	1	1	5
Florida National	2	3	9	6

Frequency of Occurrence in Top 4

Barnett Banks - 3
Sun Banks - 3
Trust Company - 3
Wachovia - 2

Our first measure of banks' current performance, the price-earnings (P/E) ratio, reflects the growth potential and risk of a company as perceived by financial markets. A high P/E ratio, relative to other companies, means that the market places a greater value on a company's potential. The ratio was calculated for each bank by dividing the current market price of the bank's stock by its trailing 12-month earnings per share. Net interest margin and return on assets, the two current profitability measures used in our analysis, are important performance indicators. The net interest margin reflects the bank's major source of income, and its return on assets measures its efficient use of total assets.

We also wanted a measure of historical performance and therefore calculated each bank's five-year compound growth rate of total assets, which measures a bank's ability to serve its customers.

We ranked each bank on a scale of one to 10 on all four criteria. Wachovia, Trust Company, Barnett Banks, and Sun Banks ranked in the top four in all categories more often than did their peers (see Table 1). Our results were confirmed by the November 1983 National Banking Survey of Chief Executive Officers.[3] CEOs from 2,000 of the largest commercial banks ranked Wachovia, Trust Company, Barnett and Sun Banks among the best-managed commercial banks in the South.

Using Bureau of Labor Statistics' (BLS) industry employment information, we selected industry groupings with significant southeastern employment (see Chart 1). We looked at four nonmanufacturing categories: wholesale and retail trade; transportation, communication and public utilities; finance, insurance and real estate; and miscellaneous services. We selected five industries from nondurable manufacturing: textiles, apparel, food and kindred products, chemicals and allied products, and paper and allied products. We also selected three durable manufacturing industries: transportation equipment, fabricated metal, and electrical and electronic equipment.

Because of the time involved, we were unable to interview all of the companies that were nominated and passed the financial screen. We instead limited ourselves to conducting interviews at 21 companies that represent a cross-section in terms of southeastern industry, geographic location, size, and age. Table 2 shows the selected companies, their industry dispersion and geographic location.

Table 3 shows the size and age of each company within the selected group. Companies chosen range in age from four to 107 years and vary in size from less than $70 million to $6.8 billion in sales. Their staffs ranged from 350 employees to almost 40,000.

Directors nominated companies based in North Carolina and South Carolina, as well as states in the Sixth Federal Reserve District—Alabama, Florida, Georgia, Louisiana, Mississippi and Tennessee.
Nominated private companies also were compared to their industry peers whenever information was available. Nissan USA in Tennessee was not subjected to the same quantitative screen. Financial information was not readily available because the new Nissan USA is a subsidiary of the larger Nissan Limited of Japan. The U.S. company was selected because of its unique position in the Southeast as a Japanese-owned

American company that has incorporated elements of Japanese-style management. Financial information for Hayes Microcomputer Products and Bank Earnings International was disclosed to us on a confidential basis.
National Banking Survey of Chief Executive Officers, November 1983, Egon Zehnder International Management Consultants, p. 11. The best-managed commercial banks in the South were ranked as follows: 1) Wachovia, 2) Texas Commerce, 3) Trust Company, 4) Barnett Banks, 5) Allied Bancshares, 6) Republic of Dallas, First Tennessee, Louisiana National, Sun Banks, United Virginia (all equally ranked).

Table 2. Industry Representation ^

Industry Group	Company	Line of Business	Geographic Location
Wholesale and Retail Trade	Home Depot	Retail lumber	Atlanta, Ga.
	Publix Super Markets	Retail grocery	Lakeland, Fla.
Miscellaneous services	Bank Earnings International	Bank Consulting	Atlanta, Ga.
	Days Inn	Hotel and motel	Atlanta, Ga.
	Charter Medical	Hospital management	Macon, Ga.
	Management Sci. Amer.	Computer software	Atlanta, Ga.
Transportation, Communication and Public Utilities	Federal Express	Express information delivery	Memphis, Tenn.
	Delta Air Lines	Airline	Atlanta, Ga.
Finance, Insurance and Real Estate	Barnett Banks of Florida	Banking	Jacksonville, Fla.
	Sun Banks	Banking	Orlando, Fla.
	Wachovia	Banking	Winston-Salem, N. C.
	Trust Company	Banking	Atlanta, Ga.
Electrical and Electronic equipment	Intelligent Systems	Computer graphics terminals	Norcross, Ga.
	Hayes Microcomputer Products	Consumer electronics	Norcross, Ga.
Transportation equipment	Nissan Motor Manuf., U. S. A.	Truck manufacturing	Smyrna, Tenn.
Fabricated metal	Nucor	Steel manufacturing	Charlotte, N. C.
Textile and apparel	Russell	Textile and apparel	Alexander City, Ala.
	Oxford Industries	Apparel	Atlanta, Ga.
Food and kindred products	Flowers Industries	Bakery products	Thomasville, Ga.
	The Coca-Cola Co.	Beverage	Atlanta, Ga.
Chemicals and allied products	Key Pharmaceuticals	Pharmaceutical	Miami, Fla.
Paper and allied products	Sonoco Products	Industrial packaging	Hartsville, S. C.

Table 3. Corporate Profiles

	Age in Years	Number of Employees 12/31/83	Sales Calendar Year 1983 ($ Mil.)	5-Year Compound Growth Rate Net Sales (%)	Return[1] on Average Assets (%) 1983	Return[1] on Average Equity (%) 1983
Nissan Motor Mfg., U. S. A.	4	1,800	5,000[2]	N. A.	N. A.	N. A.
The Home Depot	6	2,400	256[3]	125.5[4]	14.91	24.61
Hayes Microcomputer Products	6	350	N. A.[5]	N. A.[5]	N. A.[5]	N. A.[5]
Bank Earnings International	8	122	N. A.[5]	N. A.[5]	N. A.[5]	N. A.[5]
Federal Express Corp.	11	17,059	1,194[6]	44.5	10.63	20.58
Intelligent Systems	11	420	73	52.0	19.08	24.21
Days Inn of America, Inc.	14	13,500[7]	228	13.6	3.99	31.96
Charter Medical Corp.	15	8,500	375	29.5	7.18	29.44
Nucor Corp.	18	3,700	543	12.1	7.0	11.38
Management Sci. Amer., Inc.	21	1,857	145	40.8	9.10	12.29
Key Pharmaceuticals, Inc.	37	1,150	127	78.5	19.63	37.97
Oxford Industries, Inc.	42	12,884	543	17.3	12.30	23.53
Sun Banks, Inc.	50	9,200	8,901[8]	31.5[8]	0.85	14.75
Publix Super Markets, Inc.	54	33,985	2,853	11.2	11.09	17.93
Delta Air Lines, Inc.	55	37,239	3,883	12.0	−0.45[10]	−1.45[10]
Flowers Industries, Inc.	65	9,065	553	15.7	9.25	18.50
Russell Corp.	82	8,800	319	12.6	10.78	17.03
Sonoco Products Co.	85	10,008	669	14.2	9.04	14.77
Trust Company of Georgia	93	4,671	4,850[8]	12.2[8]	1.58	24.38
The Coca-Cola Co.	98	39,792	6,829[9]	10.8	11.01	19.61
Wachovia Corp.	105	6,544	7,850[8]	11.6[8]	1.20	18.41
Barnett Banks of Florida, Inc.	107	10,669	9,397[8]	24.2[8]	.98	17.94

[1] Calendar year net income divided by average assets and average shareholders' equity, respectively. Averages were calculated based on beginning and ending balances.
[2] Approximated U. S. sales
[3] Year-ending January 30, 1984.
[4] Three-year compound growth rate
[5] Privately-held company, data not available for public use.
[6] Year-ending November 30, 1983
[7] Includes approximately 6,000 franchised employees
[8] Total assets as of December 31st
[9] Worldwide
[10] Deregulation reduced returns in the airline industry in 1983.

bagging groceries, cutting meats, or operating a cash register.

One byproduct of this personal management involvement is informality. Personal involvement obviates much of the need for memos, standing committees, and procedural manuals. Many companies are simply too new to have developed procedural manuals. In such firms, autonomy and authority flow from the inculcation of corporate values and the expectations that relations between employees and management are long-term and essentially harmonious.

Another result of such patterns is a lean organizational structure. Nissan has only five levels of management above production line workers: supervisor, operations manager, plant manager, vice president, and president. In contrast, many American auto companies have 10 to 12 layers. Nucor has only 17 people at its austere headquarters in Charlotte. Flowers has only 100 people. Of course, given our focus on southeastern companies, we tended to exclude very large businesses; financial criteria, such as high growth and profit rates, also tended to draw newer companies into our sample. However, older and larger high-performance companies such as Oxford Industries and Flowers also feature lean management structures and achieve superior results through decentralization.

Decentralization. The emphasis on shared goals and values, reinforced through two-way communications and personal involvement of senior management, inculcates the entrepreneurial, action-oriented spirit throughout high-performance companies. Some businesses also foster this orientation through decentralization.

Barnett Banks of Florida, the largest bank holding company in Florida, best exemplifies such decentralization. Company officials attribute much of the bank's success to an organizational structure with grass-roots autonomy that heightens motivation for lower level management. In an environment where employees at all levels feel free to take the initiative to solve problems without first seeking approval from a higher official, often at a remote headquarters location, a "bias toward action" ensues. As a result, customers can expect faster decisions and more personalized service. Barnett stresses this aspect of its management in its advertising. Barnett officials also believe that decentralization fosters product innovation and experimentation. An idea can be tested on a small scale without central approval; if successful, it

can be adopted elsewhere in the system. Barnett's cash management and its program to market to consumers planning to move to Florida came from banks within the system, not from headquarters.

Each of Charter's hospital managers is responsible for the budget and profits of his operation. Charter Medical's CEO William Fickling hires "compulsive overachievers" and gives them free rein. He not only leaves the operational details to others in the company; he allows subordinates to pursue policies or directions that he believes may be misguided. Oxford and Nucor employ the single business unit concept: each division is responsible for its own marketing, manufacturing, budgeting, planning, plant, equipment, and personnel. Similarly, each of Sonoco's five divisions operates as a profit center. In Flowers' system of specialized plants, each bakery produces items needed by other Flowers bakeries in its region. Thus, each plant must stand on its own profitability as if it were an independent company.

Not all successful companies are decentralizing. Charter Medical dissolved three regional headquarters on the grounds that the company's size could not justify the overhead costs. Even some of the intrinsically decentralized retail companies centralize many functions. Home Depot's store managers control only personnel matters; pricing, advertising, and purchasing are handled centrally. Federal Express's station managers are not expected to be creative. The company's success is predicated upon uniform quality.

Nonetheless, many action-oriented companies try to delegate responsibility and thereby avoid the bureaucratic mentality of following rules imposed by someone else in the organization. Employees at most companies we studied are encouraged to solve problems in a way that best fits the corporate mission and value structure. At Nissan, production teams practice consensus decision-making among peers rather than seeking a ruling from top management. Managers who had formerly worked at U. S. automobile companies told us, "We solve problems across the table here, rather than up and down the chain of command." When decisions are made by the people who are most affected, the result can be quicker and more flexible actions. Leland Strange, CEO of Intelligent Systems, emphasizes each employee's responsibility for action: "The only way our employees get in trouble with us is to not be doing something, not taking action. They'll never get in trouble for doing the wrong thing if they use a reasonable, rational process to get there."

Creating an atmosphere free from recrimination also fosters the spread of an entrepreneurial spirit. Sonoco's Coker takes ultimate responsibility for acquisitions recommended by various managers. If an acquisition proves less successful than anticipated, the managers are not blamed. There is a certain risk in telling others of a problem or of calling off a project in which the company has invested heavily, but companies in our sample encourage such forthrightness. These companies do not "kill the messenger who brings the bad news." Marvin Runyon tells his employees, "Never stay in trouble by yourself." By telling others about a problem, it can be corrected before it becomes insurmountable.

Few Perquisites. Incentives are intended to foster action, decisions, and risk-taking; therefore, high-performance companies consciously avoid perquisites based on status and seniority rather than performance. Nissan and Nucor have no reserved parking spaces for officers. Both Federal Express and Nucor restrict management vacations to conform with those allowed employees. No management personnel at Federal Express may take vacation during the Christmas holidays since employees must work during these periods. Federal Express has no executive dining room. There are no offices at Hayes Microcomputer Products. Everyone, including the CEO, works in a cubicle open at the top and with no door. Nissan offers discounted auto leases on Nissan trucks to all employees, not just to managers. CEO Marvin Runyon wears the company's standard blue coveralls, issued to all employees.

This sensitivity does not imply that these companies are worker democracies, although they do give employees opportunities to participate in decision-making. Managers are rewarded well, typically through stock options and bonuses based on return on assets. Days Inn offers limited partnerships to rising managers. Moreover, the reduction or redistribution of status symbols does not imply a social egalitarianism. Neither a woman nor a black was among the 100 or so executive officers we interviewed. In several manufacturing facilities, women hold the lowest positions and seemed to have little hope of career advancement. At Nissan and Nucor, however, women held high-paying, traditionally male jobs, such as welding. Moreover, opportunities

for disadvantaged groups seem promising because most high-performance companies emphasize treating all employees fairly.[3]

Cohesiveness. A final action-fostering management characteristic, and one that surprised us initially, was the stress on cohesiveness, especially among top management. CEOs seek to build such a cadre because they believe it enhances the entrepreneurial spirit. Wachovia uses the analogy of a basketball team. If the players know one another well, they can gain an intuitive sense of what to expect of their colleagues and thus act faster. Kessler of Days Inn typified this outlook with his comment: "Management is at its best when it is of similar mind, spirit, and objective." Many companies are led by graduates of the same college. Georgia Tech alumni predominate at Days Inn and MSA. Many of the top officers at Sonoco have known each other most of their lives. The average tenure of senior management at Wachovia is 20 years. At Federal Express, Fred Smith urges participation from below. Chief operating officer Jim Barksdale says the reason he got the job is because he could "take Fred on." Yet other officers say they feel lucky if they come away with a draw in a confrontation with Smith.

Some companies encourage dissent and diversity. Debate and dissent flourish at Barnett, not just within the circle of top management but in larger meetings that include board members and stockholders. MSA recruits a diverse work force, ranging from extroverted sales people to creative computer specialists, who write software, and nurturing employees who help sustain the company's reputation for customer service. The company tries to hire a diversity of educational backgrounds, including music majors as well as those trained in math and computer science. Company leaders value debate. At a company meeting of 30 people, a manager rose after President Bill Graves' presentation and told him, in so many words, that the idea Graves had advanced was ridiculous. The manager was subsequently promoted to an officer, in large part because of his willingness to stand up for what he believes. Of course, MSA officials note that dissent must remain in the realm of ideas; employees at all levels are expected to comply in action with company policies until they can convince others through the persuasiveness of their arguments of the need for change.

More typically, we found a collegiality in decision-making within the companies' somewhat homogeneous management teams. Sonoco's CEO describes himself as an "orchestrator" who solicits ideas from other senior managers rather than originating all strategies himself. Nucor's Iverson characterizes himself as more of an arbiter at the company's regular group managers meetings, where key decisions are made. Sun Banks called on the assistance of 100 people to formulate its mission statement and attendant strategy and tactics.

Many CEOs express concern about the lack of dissent and divergence. The longevity of management and the commonality of backgrounds may serve to insulate the organization and create a need for self-renewal at times. Once a company has achieved success, it becomes harder to maintain the reputation of excellence than it was to build it. Coca-Cola finds complacency a major concern as do Wachovia and MSA. Donald Keough at Coke said, "You have to keep providing opportunities for people to enjoy the thrill of victory. When you've been on a winning team for so long, the motivation becomes the fear of losing rather than the thrill of winning." Coca-Cola responded to this challenge when Roberto Goizueta took the helm in 1980. Although his new management team consists of long-term Coke employees, they have established a new strategy and sense of direction. Division and country managers have been encouraged to contribute their views to policies and decisions in a way that had long been absent at Coke. The new spirit instituted by Goizueta is reflected in the spate of new products Coca-Cola has introduced in the last three years, in the company's willingness to rely more heavily on debt financing than in the past, and in its commitment to retain a higher portion of earnings for reinvestment rather than for distribution as dividends to stockholders.

For many managers, the entrepreneurial spirit is renewed when a series of events threatens the company's success or even survival. Wachovia redirected itself in the early 1970s. Flowers, Sonoco, and Oxford realized the need for a change as their industries matured and began declining. Days Inn pulled through a tough period in the mid-1970s by demanding emphasis on quality control. The memories of these times are still vivid in the minds of senior management. Many have vowed never to "get fat, dumb, and happy" again.

The fact that we found an entrepreneurial style of management operating in new companies, sustained in older firms, and renewed in businesses that had lost it gave us reason to believe that this style and the mechanisms that support it—corporate mission, communications, personal involvement, and participative decision-making—are important in the corporate successes we studied.

Affiliation of Employees

Viewing their companies as social institutions, families, or teams leads management of high-performance firms to look on their employees as integral affiliates rather than as adversaries or commodities. Employees at high-performance companies often exhibit the same "fired up" enthusiasm as members of winning sports teams. Since workers are viewed as family members, they do not seem to seek an outside party, such as a union, to represent their interests. Unions were noticeably absent at these companies, even those in highly unionized industries.

Profit-Based Rewards. This familial view of employees is, in most cases, distinct from the paternalism that prevailed historically in certain industries and areas. Workers are treated with respect. Nissan refers to its assembly-line workers as technicians. Employees at Nissan and elsewhere are paid well, especially in comparison to industry or local standards. Moreover, their remuneration is usually based on the same criteria as that of management. Nucor's employees receive weekly and yearly bonuses based on their division's return on assets. There is no upper limit to this. The $30,000 median income of steelworkers at Nucor's Darlington, S. C. mill is far higher than local income norms.[4] Stock ownership by employees is widespread, although stock purchase plans outnumber plans based solely on employer contributions. Charter Medical, Federal Express, Nucor, and Sun Banks are among the companies with stock purchase plans. Key Pharmaceuticals, Publix, and Intelligent Systems have employee stock ownership plans.[5] Coca-Cola is implementing a stock ownership plan in stages so that many of its employees will become shareholders on retirement.

Profit-sharing plans also are fairly common. For example, 20 percent of Publix's profits go to employees and another 15 percent go to an employee retirement fund. Similarly, Nucor has

The Case-Study Approach: Advantages and Problems

Having identified high-performance companies in the region, we spent six months conducting case studies to identify common management characteristics. Our case studies began with intensive scrutiny of annual and 10-K reports, studies by securities analysts, and other published literature for each company. Then our team of researchers conducted day-long interviews with senior management, touring operations, and, in some cases, meeting with employees.

We chose this in-depth approach, encompassing a smaller sample, rather than the broad swath of respondents typically covered by a survey, for several reasons. The case-study method has been used extensively in social science research, particularly in anthropology, psychology, and, to some extent, in political science. It is the primary method of analysis used by such premier business schools as Harvard, Stanford, and the University of Virginia, which promote excellence in the management of business. We felt this approach was appropriate to our research.

Another factor motivating our choice was our concern with the problem of response set bias. This phenomenon, whereby most respondents try to give positive answers that they believe the researcher wishes to find, distorts the results of attitude surveys. Although careful phrasing of questions can help counter the human trait to please, we felt that the popularity of recent books on this subject would make it difficult to overcome this tendency.

We felt it was necessary to interview a variety of top officers and, in some cases, workers in the companies we were sampling to determine whether adherence to principles was more than rhetoric. Through interviews, our panel of four researchers—who have diverse academic and professional backgrounds—were able to probe and discover patterns that could not be discerned through a questionnaire. Some of those interviewed pointed out aspects of currently popular management literature they considered completely incorrect. Others voiced initial agreement with certain management principles, but the ensuing interchange suggested that such principles were either not borne out in fact or were of minor importance in their organization.

Using a research team helped us address another problem of certain types of survey research, that of intercoder reliability. Some surveys utilize more open-ended questions that allow respondents greater opportunity to phrase answers in an idiosyncratic and presumably more sincere manner. Tallying or finding

patterns in answers to such open-ended questions involves an evaluation by the researcher who codes responses in accordance with a preconceived set of answers or a typology. Different researchers may code the same document in a variety of ways. By using the case-study approach, with several researchers present at each interview, we could test the correctness of our evaluation of interviewee comments by discussing them with one another.

A final problem this methodology addressed better than that of survey research was that of validity—do the indicators really measure the variables and hypotheses being tested? Certainly, we cannot be sure that because top management and a handful of employees told us a company placed a high value on its staff, that it did in fact do so in general. On the other hand, we are much more certain of the validity of the responses we got because of the opportunity to talk at length with more than one respondent at each firm—including those most responsible for the conduct of the company.

This study is subject to certain limitations. The most important is that we are not unequivocally certain that these principles are in fact correlated with the financial success of the companies under study. Many of the policies we have reported have been implemented only recently. We, along with most of the corporate officials we interviewed, believe such a relationship exists. Yet it remains for subsequent research to examine this issue further. Second, we cannot be certain that the management principles related to us by senior officers are in fact being implemented in the way they claim or believe. However, plant tours, our conversations with employees, and the strong objections voiced by many company leaders regarding certain characteristics we expected to find lead us to believe that the principles do obtain in practice. Third, our findings seem more prominent or consistent at new or rising entrepreneurial companies than at long-established and historically successful companies for which stewardship is a prominent value. Fourth, our focus on southeastern companies might incorporate a regional bias. Because the area's traditional comparative advantage has been low-cost labor, for example, attitudes toward technology and human resource optimization might be somewhat less pronounced than in other sections of the country. Despite these potential limitations, we believe our study has validity and bears policy implications both for the private and public sector.

no fixed pension plan but rather a deferred profit-sharing plan that will produce retirement income for the company's 3,600 employees only if it continues to succeed financially. Days Inn recently instituted Day Cap, a thrift plan, whereby the company matches employee savings by 25 percent or more, depending on annual profits. To participate, employees must contribute at least 2 percent of their wages or salaries. Wachovia has a savings incentive plan that allows employees to contribute up to 6 percent of their salaries. The company matches from 50 to over 100 percent of employee contributions, according to annual performance in meeting profitability targets. Trust Company offers an incentive compensation plan, whereby all employees with at least three years tenure receive a bonus of as much as 20 percent of their pay. The bonus is based on both the performance of the company as a whole and the individual's bank. Flowers offers bonus, incentive, and stock purchase programs; employees are informed weekly of their plant's profitability, its attainment of operating goals, and areas requiring improvement.

In these plans, employee compensation or retirement benefits are linked directly to the company's profitability. These plans also are similar in deriving from group rather than individual performance. Like the owner, employees can not succeed through excellent individual performance alone; the group—whether a work station of 20 people, a unit bank, or a corporate division—must prosper for the individual to gain.

Employees: Long-Term Corporate Assets. Employees at high-performance companies are regarded as the firm's most important long-term asset, not a cheap resource that is easily replaced. Delta officials believe job security is critical in sustaining employee commitment. Delta has not furloughed workers since 1956. Nucor and Nissan, among others, avoid laying people off. Nucor has not laid off an employee in 15 years; in hard times all workers go on short hours. Since employees are regarded as a quasi-permanent investment, high-performance companies place great importance on recruiting. Many companies intentionally locate in rural areas where few employers will compete with them in hiring the best applicants. Nissan, Nucor, and Oxford have been most successful in this regard. Nucor recently received 1,400 applicants for nine openings. Nissan had 130,000 applicants for 1,800 positions.

Some companies prefer to hire employees with no previous experience in the industry so that they can instill the company's values from the outset. At Charter Medical, for example, officers like to hire hospital administrators fresh out of school and then "Charterize" them. Nucor and Nissan have few workers with previous experience in the steel or auto industries.

Some companies look not just to individual employees as long-term corporate assets, but to their families as well. Key Pharmaceuticals prides itself on having 13 members of one family. Flowers offers scholarships and summer jobs for children of employees and boasts of its second-generation workers. Nucor provides partial-tuition reimbursement to children of employees; in return they must attend several company meetings, write an analysis of the annual report, and consider Nucor as a potential employer upon graduation.

Training. Since they view employees as their most important long-term assets, high-performance firms offer substantial training opportunities. Sun Banks employees at a variety of grade levels can improve their career prospects while remaining with the company by attending Sun Banks University. Sun Banks attempts to identify, train, and advance what it calls "mustangs," employees with great promise but insufficient education to fulfill their potential. Moreover, Sun Banks has a formal mentoring system: everyone from the assistant manager level up is assigned to a senior officer. Nucor pays for the training of employees who successfully post for vacancies within a mill. Nissan's employees go through pre-employment training, funded by the state of Tennessee, before being hired. They continue to have access to a variety of machines and instruction facilities in order to advance to other jobs to develop a pool of candidates for future leadership. Home Depot officers train middle managers; Sonoco and Flowers also have extensive training for management and supervisors.

Flexibility. Another aspect related to training is job flexibility or enrichment. Most companies we interviewed rotate their employees through a variety of tasks, particularly those whose work tends to be monotonous or unpleasant. For example, Days Inn's chambermaids also work as waitresses, Key Pharmaceuticals' production-line workers, who watch bottles to make sure labels have been affixed properly, rotate every two hours to perform other activities. At Nissan every chassis division worker must learn all 19 skills involved in this stage of the assembly process. This flexibility benefits the company by expanding the supply of labor able to perform any given task and gives the employee a larger perspective regarding the company.

The latter is an important point. Although most companies we visited attempt to make working for the company more fulfilling, they make no pretense about the nature of some jobs. Work at many of the companies is far from utopian. However, most of these companies try to mitigate the effects of unpleasant tasks.

Participation. Another common characteristic at high-performance companies is a greater opportunity for participation. In addition to two-way communications, companies we studied offer opportunities for employee peer groups to meet on their own. At Oxford, for example, job enrichment groups meet regularly to discuss ways to improve production and other job-related matters. This is the closest to quality circles we discovered. Even Nissan has not yet instituted this element of Japanese management. Employees at Charter, Federal Express, and Oxford are polled frequently regarding their supervisors. Managers at Federal and Oxford who consistently receive negative remarks from subordinates are not promoted. Trust Company and Sun Banks recently surveyed their employees about their job satisfaction and instituted policy changes as a result.

Market Strategy

Judging from our research, clearly defined market strategy seems to stem from a well-understood and well-focused corporate mission. In refining this strategy, management has asked: What can we do well? What is our comparative advantage relative to other companies in the business? What unmet market needs can we satisfy? What additional expertise must we develop?

Niches. The answers to these questions have led most high-performance companies to seek a market niche—a well-defined segment of a much larger market. "Niching" limits the competition and allows companies with good quality and low costs to dominate a market segment. Some companies create a niche by identifying and serving an unmet need. Key Pharmaceuticals found a niche among pharmaceutical giants by

developing new ways to administer proven drugs. Federal Express provided a totally new service— delivering time-sensitive business documents and equipment parts point to point within 24 hours at a relatively low cost.

High Value-Added. Companies competing in the lower-cost end of the market try to distinguish themselves by offering better quality than their competitors. To provide that extra level of quality at reasonable prices, the company must contain costs. Days Inn seeks to provide high quality, low-cost lodgings by choosing simple, no-frills, yet attractive, designs. Home Depot reduces costs and adds value through its retail-warehouse concept, while offering a larger variety and stock of products. Russell's new marketing effort promises customers high quality athletic wear, such as warm-up suits and jogging shorts, at lower-than-designer-label prices.

Companies serving the higher-priced end of the market are able to create a demand based on the perceived quality or value of the product. Trust Company emphasizes its return on assets, one of the best among American banks. It seeks high caliber customers, not the greatest volume. As one officer states, "Trust Company does not give away dishes." Barnett raises such standard financial services as auto installment loans above the level of a commodity by making its service faster and more dependable. Barnett's staff can approve a car loan request from a dealer in an hour at most. In addition, unlike many banks, it continues auto lending even when interest rates are abnormally high. In general, Barnett tries to avoid selling only commodity financial products like IRAs. Instead it encourages employees to know their local market as a whole and how best to respond to it. Oxford Industries improved its financial performance by shifting from manufacturing for mass market retailers to producing designer and specialty label sportswear. When a competitor lowered its prices, Federal Express responded by raising prices and improving its delivery time from noon to 10:30 a.m. on next-day service. Sonoco locates its plants near customers to ensure reliable delivery. It distinguishes its commodity-like paper products by offering consistent availability and designs tailored to the customer's needs.

Market Share. Some high-performance companies are driven by market share, constantly trying to gain a larger share of the pie by taking business from competitors rather than by seeking to increase demand. This strategy contrasts with trying to make the pie larger by creating a greater demand with new and innovative products. When the pie stops growing and market share has reached a high point, it is difficult to generate much growth in the company. This phenomenon occurred in the beverage industry. Once driven solely by increasing the volume of soft drink sales, Coca-Cola is now looking for new opportunities in new markets.

In some cases, demographics, deregulation, or technological breakthroughs expand the market "pie" dramatically. Florida's banking industry is growing because almost 1,000 people move into the state each day. Barnett and Sun Banks are striving to increase market share, although quality of service and innovative product lines are also important to them. Publix also benefits from the growing Florida population and makes its goal to blanket the state with new stores.

Oxford's primary business is designing, manufacturing, and selling consumer apparel products. Sonoco's is manufacturing and selling industrial packaging products. However, within those broad definitions, the two companies dominate several niches. In addition to supplying the textile industry with almost all of the paper and plastic cones used to wind yarn, Sonoco is one of the few suppliers of the new plastic grocery bags. Oxford has the exclusive rights to produce and sell several designer lines. While Russell's business is sportswear, it also specializes in team uniforms.

Product Integrity. We found several principles that guide companies in selecting and implementing market strategies. A prominent one is: they "stick to their knitting." Acquisitions and new market niches fit closely with their current mix of business. Sonoco seeks companies that complement its existing lines. For example, a byproduct from one division may be used as a resource for another division. Federal Express' ground delivery system complements its move into facsimile transmission of documents. Federal Express will be able to pick up a customer's document and deliver it by truck to a processing center, which will use image technology and satellite communications to transmit it to another city. Flowers uses its efficient distribution system, which was established to deliver fresh-baked bread daily, to deliver the snack foods it has

begun producing. Its acquisitions are primarily in snack foods because of the higher margins, but the company realizes the importance of increasing market share in its "bread and butter" business - loaf bread. Iverson transformed Nucor from a money-losing hodgepodge of miscellaneous products into a company focusing almost solely on low-cost steel production. Coke has in the past three years brought more continuity to its product line by divesting subsidiaries such as Aqua-Chem and Tenco, which were not marketing to individuals, and by acquiring Columbia Pictures and Ronco, both of which market directly to consumers.

Wachovia cut back its data services subsidiary and divested itself of a credit business, a courier company, an insurance agency, and a title insurance agency in the early 1970s. John Medlin says, "We have rededicated ourselves to being the very best bank we know how to be and to sticking with the basic corporate, retail, trust, and money market services that are permitted to a bank." When Wachovia was highly diversified, its compound earnings growth rate was 10 percent a year. Since the redirection, earnings have compounded at 19 percent annually. Medlin says, "You shouldn't acquire things that you can't manage and don't understand and don't know how to run."

Long-term orientation. Another marketing principle of high-performance companies is a long-term orientation. These companies look for consistent growth and profitability. Flowers, for instance, looks to long-term growth when it buys failing bakeries and spends liberally to modernize them. Closely-held ownership of many of these companies enhances corporate leaders' freedom to retain an orientation to longer-term instead of quarterly profits. William Fickling of Charter Medical, for instance, holds most of the voting stock of his company. Sonoco, Russell, and Flowers are closely held by family members, with only a small portion of their stock traded by institutional investors. Russell's chief financial officer says the company prefers to keep it that way to avoid constant "looking over your shoulder" by the investment community.

Service to Customers. Most companies in our study believe their mission is to serve their customers' needs. Nissan's production line employees are kept in touch with the people

Exhibit 1.

	1	**2**	**3**	**4**
Technology/Innovation	No original innovation, copies innovative activity of others after proven successful	Innovates with high degree of caution	Innovates extensively after careful analysis	Innovation is lifeblood of organization
Entrepreneurial Management	Bureaucratic hierarchical structure breeds passivity; focus of action on "turf battles"	Leadership acts in response to crisis & to catch-up to competitors	Leadership takes risks; employees execute but do not originate	Participation spreads action-orientation throughout organization
Affiliation of Employees	Meets basic human needs, but views human resources as a commodity	Develops human resources to limited degree	Develops human resources extensively	Human potential is developed as major corporate investment
Market Strategy	Maintains stable market share	Participates in some new markets, and increases share of existing markets	Participates extensively in new markets	Creates new markets

Tracking the Patterns: A Spectrum

Technology and innovation constitute the lifeblood of some organizations. Change is constant. These companies' markets are fast-growing, and relevant technologies are evolving rapidly. Other companies find innovation and technology necessary to their businesses, but they emphasize feasibility rather than innovation for its own sake. Some companies are cautious toward innovation but are willing to embrace change when the benefits are evident. The far left end of the spectrum holds companies whose strategy is to copy the innovative activity of others once it has proven successful.

Entrepreneurial management is most pronounced at companies with a strong sense of purpose and identity and participative decision-making style that fosters debate, autonomy, and initiative. At firms with a less entrepreneurial management style, middle managers and employees are kept well-informed of company policies and performance, but they merely implement decisions made at the top. At other companies action is undertaken usually in response to outside crises, and less emphasis is placed on informing lower level managers and employees of company philosophy, policies, or changes in these. Finally, in bureaucratically managed businesses, entrepreneurship is inhibited by a hierarchical structure that breeds passivity and conformity to rules and traditions. Energy is focused more on rivals within the organization than on competitors in the market.

Human resources are utilized most effectively in companies that seek to develop employees to their fullest potential. They consider their employees investments that can leverage the company's hard assets. Other companies emphasize developing and training employees, but do not see that as the major way to improve productivity. In less people-oriented companies, employees may be treated fairly but there is limited fulfillment through jobs. Finally, some companies meet the basic human needs, but view labor as an easily replaceable commodity.

Some companies expand by finding new, unexploited markets. These are the entrepreneurs in the truest sense of the word. Others participate in existing growth markets and some new markets. Some companies grow by increasing their market share in stable markets and by limited participation in new markets. Others merely try to maintain stable market share in existing businesses.

Each of four researchers in our group ranked the companies on a continuum of TEAM characteristics (Exhibit 1). According to our scale, the perfect TEAM company would receive a rating of 16: four points were awarded when a characteristic was strongly present; one point implied a weak presence of the trait. This rating method, although subjective, provides a useful benchmark for comparison.

We encourage the reader to score his or her company on its performance of the TEAM characteristics. If the total score is lower than the average (13 points for all the high-performance companies we visited), our findings suggest some of the measures employed by high performance companies might be beneficial.

they serve by means of displays at each work station quoting customer and dealer comments. Sonoco's production employees occasionally visit customer sites to see how their products are used. At some Sun Banks, tellers are given a quarter every time they call a customer by name. Barnett's employees receive $5.00 for selling a credit card to a customer; having a customer fill out an application earns them $1.00.

At many firms senior officers are required to keep in touch with the market directly. At Federal Express each top officer has personal responsibility for at least one major sales account, which he must visit regularly. Sonoco customers work with company engineers to design product innovations and refinements. MSA awards special status, in addition to the typical financial remuneration, to high-performing sales people. Prestige awards include King's Court, Tiger's Club, and President's Council. Winners take vacation trips with the company's senior management and carry special ID cards marked with their elite affiliation. Perhaps Bank Earnings, Inc. is the ultimate in serving the customer. When they go into a bank to offer their advice on cutting costs in the bank's operations, they are generally paid with a proportion of the first year of savings resulting from BEI's efforts. Basically, the accountants at the client and the consultant agree on how this should be measured. "We don't even talk in terms of how many days it will take our team to do a job," says President Jerry Eickhoff. "That's our problem. We promise certain results, regardless of how long it takes to get them. And those results are defined in terms of the client's satisfaction, not ours. We can't afford to have unhappy clients running around, so we do everything we can to give them a quality job."

Conclusions

Technological innovation, participative management, respect for employees, and carefully defined market strategies are qualities shared by our sample of successful southeastern companies. The corporate characteristics we have designated as the TEAM approach are emphasized more by some high-performance companies than others. It would be unfair to say that the elements we are highlighting are appropriate in every business situation. Moreover, the four TEAM characteristics exist within each company in a variety of mixtures. For example, some companies have invested heavily in technological innovation, but have yet to discover the importance of their human capital. We found it useful to picture each trait along a continuum (see box on "Tracking the Patterns").

Nonetheless because we found patterns across industry lines, in both old and new companies, in manufacturing and services, in high tech and low tech, in large and small companies, we believe the management principles we have identified apply broadly. Moreover, many measures involve little capital infusion. Respectful treatment of employees and participative management techniques cost little and may reduce costs during economic downturns. Thus, the implications of this study for the private sector are positive.

The implications for public policy are more complex. Many programs now pursued by state economic development agencies seem irrelevant to the principles discerned through our investigation. Virtually no officials mentioned favorable state and local tax treatment as a critical factor in their company's start up or success. One important exception seems to be state programs that provide funding to train labor for facilities locating in the state. High-performance businesses consider employee training an important function. This study calls into question whether such programs should be limited to new businesses coming into the state; perhaps state-sponsored training programs

should be extended to existing firms wishing to improve their performance by upgrading workers. Programs might also be expanded to help managers and supervisors implement a more participative management style. Many companies we visited had such programs in-house, and others noted the difficulties of having managers accept the full spirit of this style.

The main implication of this study is that a primary goal of economic development policies should be creating a climate conducive to developing and nourishing the entrepreneur. The entrepreneur who develops the kind of people-oriented companies discussed in this study provides a model for innovation and sustained high performance.

—Donald L. Koch
Delores W. Steinhauser,
Bobbie H. McCrackin
and Kathryn Hart

Notes

[1] Donald L. Koch, William N. Cox, Delores W. Steinhauser and Pamela V. Whigham, "High Technology: The Southeast Reaches Out For Growth Industry," **Economic Review**, Federal Reserve Bank of Atlanta (September 1983), pp. 4-19.
[2] "Commodities" refer to highly uniform, usually mass-produced, goods.
[3] Most companies attribute this absence to the fairly recent entry of women and minorities into management ranks. As they build up experience, they say, such employees are likely to be selected for top positions.
[4] In Darlington County, South Carolina, where Nucor is located, the average per capita income is less than $7,000 a year.
[5] Some Intelligent Systems employees have accumulated 40,000 shares of stock, worth about $64,000 at recent prices. Corporate officers link this benefit and the longer-term commitment of its employees, a rarity in the computer industry where rapid turnover is the norm.
[6] Publication deadlines prevented our including HBO & Company. HBO is an Atlanta-based firm that designs, sells and services hospital information

systems used to monitor and analyze billing costs, patient information, and drug and laboratory data. HBO stands out as an example of the beneficial results of decentralization. Although HBO has only 600 employees, it has six regional offices that include the majority of the company's work force. This arrangement, company officials believe, gives customers better service and employees more autonomy, thus improving productivity.

In addition, recognizing that we may have missed some important characteristics of smaller financial institutions by limiting our sample to the ten largest in the Southeast, we selected First Railroad & Banking Company of Georgia in Augusta from our list of directors' nominations. The $1.5 billion in assets holding company is a medium-size financial institution whose most outstanding characteristic is its decentralized, autonomous management structure. Subsidiaries are loosely associated through the holding company; they share information and ideas through task forces and teams, and are held accountable to a financial plan.

BIBLIOGRAPHY

Abernathy, William J., Clark, Kim B. and Kantrow, Alan M. **Industrial Renaissance: Producing a Competitive Future for America,** New York: Basic Books, 1983.
American Business Conference, "The Winning Performance of Mid-sized Growth Companies," May 1983.
Drucker, Peter F. **Toward the Next Economics, and Other Essays,** New York: Harper and Row, 1981.
Grove, Andrew S. **High Output Management,** New York: Random House, 1983.
Henderson, Bruce D. **Henderson on Corporate Strategy,** New York: New American Library, 1982.
Kanter, Rosabeth Moss. **The Change Masters: Innovation for Productivity in the American Corporation,** New York: Simon and Schuster, 1983.
March, John. "Entrepreneurship," Harvard Business School **Bulletin** (February 1984), pp. 59-67.
McFarlan, Warren, and McKenney, James. **Corporate Information Systems Management: The Issues Facing Senior Executives,** Homewood, Illinois: R. D. Irwin, 1983.

Odiorne, George S. **Management Decisions by Objectives,** Englewood Cliffs, New Jersey: Prentice Hall, 1969.
Ouichi, William. **Theory Z: How American Business Can Meet the Japanese Challenge,** Reading, Massachusetts: Addison-Wesley, 1981.
Pascale, Richard T. **The Art of Japanese Management,** New York: Simon & Schuster, 1981.
Peters, Thomas J., and Waterman, Jr., Robert H. **In Search of Excellence: Lessons from America's Best-Run Companies,** New York: Harper and Row, 1982.
David A. Silver, **The Entrepreneurial Life,** New York: John Wiley & Sons, 1983.
Valle, Jacques. **The Network Revolution: Confessions of a Computer Scientist,** Berkeley, California: and/or Press, 1982.
Weil, Ulric. **Information Systems in the 80's: Products, Markets, and Vendors,** Englewood Cliffs, New Jersey: Prentice-Hall, 1982.

How to Compete Beyond the 1980s: Conference Registration

Abrams, Bernard W., Abrams Industries, Inc.
Adler, Celia G., Celia Adler Real Estate
Ahrens, Karen, Federal Reserve Bank of Atlanta
Armstrong, James C., Trust Company of Georgia
Avery, Tom A., Robinson Humphrey/American Express, Inc.
Ballard, Jerry, Jerry Ballard Homes, Inc.
Bassett, Gene, *The Atlanta Journal*
Bassler, Wardlyn, Federal Reserve Bank of Atlanta
Bedwell, Donald E., Federal Reserve Bank of Atlanta
Bosch, Mary P., Georgia Power Company
Box, James, L., First Georgia Bank
Bradfield, Betty, Federal Reserve Bank of Atlanta
Brady, Colin S., Portals, Inc.
Brandt, Harry, Federal Reserve Bank of Atlanta
Brannen, Stephen J., University of Georgia
Brinkman, Richard, Harry Norman Realtors
Brown, James S., National Bank of Sarasota
Buford, Ed R., Temtex Industries, Inc.
Bulterman, Charles L., KLM Royal Dutch Airlines
Burke, Franklin L., Bank South, N.A.
Caldwell, W. Ronnie, Federal Reserve Bank of Atlanta
Campbell, Jim, Harry Norman Realtors
Cardell, W. D., Georgia Power Company
Carefoot, George H., Florida National Bank (Tallahassee)
Carter, Charlie, Federal Reserve Bank of Atlanta
Cavallaro, Ernest A., Codisco, Inc.
Cavin, F. G., First American Corporation
Chapnick, Barry, Commonwealth Savings
Cheek, Ben F., First Franklin Financial Corporation
Cleaver, Joe M., Florida National Bank

Cleckley, John, Federal Reserve Bank of Atlanta
Cochran, Barbara, Barclays American Business Credit, Inc.
Conklin, C. S., Trust Company Bank of Clayton County
Cornish, Cheryl L., Federal Reserve Bank of Atlanta
Cox, William N., Federal Reserve Bank of Atlanta
Craig, Sara V., Social Security Administration
Craven, Frank, Federal Reserve Bank of Atlanta
Crossnine, Raymond, Social Security Administration
Currey, Bradley, Rock-Tenn Company
Daniels, Michael J., Columbus College, Small Business Development Center
Darrah, James D., BellSouth Corporation
Davis, Bob, Texas Tech University
Deeley, Anne, Deeley/Fenton & Associates, Inc.
Demer, James, Social Security Administration
Dingler, Melinda, Federal Reserve Bank of Atlanta
Duer, Thomas C., Sun Banks, Inc.
Dunlap, Tully F., Ellis Bank & Trust Company
Dyer, J. David, Jr., First Federal Savings and Loan Association
Eaves, Randall, First National Bank of Haralson County
Edwards, Randy, Blue Cross and Blue Shield of Georgia/Columbus, Inc.
Eickhoff, Gerald, Bank Earnings International
Eickhoff, M. Kathryn, Townsend-Greenspan
Ekern, Philip, First National Bank of Cobb County
Epstein, Eugene, New York Stock Exchange
Erdevig, Eleanor H., Federal Reserve Bank of Chicago
Fickling, William A., Charter Medical Corporation
Ford, Basil H., Engraph, Inc.
Forrestal, Robert P., Federal Reserve Bank of Atlanta
Foster, Kevin D., ALCOA
Francis, Ronald H., The Chattahoochee Bank
Gaylord, James F., Federal Reserve Bank of Philadelphia
Gill, Daniel D., Professional Bankcorp
Ginden, Charles B., Trust Company Bank
Green, Roberta, Federal Reserve Bank of New York
Gribbin, David G., Emanuel County Junior College
Griffin, W. D., Jr., Rock-Tenn Company
Griffis, T. L., Georgia Power Company
Guerin, Robert A., Jr., Wells Fargo Armored Service Corporation
Guynn, Jack, Federal Reserve Bank of Atlanta
Hall, George H., The Georgia Bank & Trust Company
Hall, Lenvil R., Vista Banks, Inc.
Hargett, Billy H., Federal Reserve Bank of Atlanta

Harris, Linda, Federal Reserve Bank of Atlanta
Harrison, Delmar, Federal Reserve Bank of Atlanta
Hart, Kathryn, Federal Reserve Bank of Atlanta
Hartman, Jeri, Federal Reserve Bank of Atlanta
Hartmann, Bruce, Tennessee State University
Hedrick, David E., Central Bank of Volusia County
Hofmann, Peter K., P. K. Hofmann and Associates, Inc.
Hollis, Mark C., Publix Super Markets, Inc.
Howell, Jann C., Citizens and Southern Georgia Corporation
Hutcheson, Hazel T., Emanuel County Junior College
Jackson, Ethyl, Federal Reserve Bank of Atlanta
Jackson, Robert F., The First National Bank of Opelika
Jacobsen, Thomas H., Barnett Banks of Florida, Inc.
James, John B., The Citizens and Southern National Bank
Johnson, Willis, Trust Company of Georgia
Johnston, W. F., First United Corporation
Jones, Charles M., Consolidated Loan Company
Jones, Gene K., Georgia Southwestern College
Jost, Robert R., Ball State University
Kanter, Rosabeth Moss, Yale University
Kantrow, Alan M., *The Harvard Business Review*
Kimbrough, Anne, *The Atlanta Constitution*
King, Becky, *Atlanta Women's News*
Kittrell, Fred J., Middle Tennessee University
Kline, Duane, Federal Reserve Bank of Atlanta
Koch, Donald L., Federal Reserve Bank of Atlanta
Kuglar, Larry T., First National Bank of Polk County
Langley, David, *Dutch Business Press*
Lawrence, J. D., Georgia Southwestern College
Leonard, William B., Sunniland Bank
Leslie, Henry A., Union Bank and Trust Company
Lieberman, William J., Savannah Bank and Trust Company
Lilly, Janice, BellSouth Corporation
Lloyd, William S., Community Bankshares, Inc. (Cornelia Bank)
Lubitz, Mitch, St. Petersburg (Fla.) *Evening Independent*
Mallory, Randall A., MAG Mutual Insurance Company
Manion, Lori, Federal Reserve Bank of Atlanta
Marcus, Bernard, The Home Depot
Martin, Preston, Board of Governors of the Federal Reserve System
Matteri, Ely S., Federal Reserve Bank of Atlanta
McCommon, Robert L., Jr., Georgianna Products, Inc.
McCrackin, Bobbie, Federal Reserve Bank of Atlanta
McKeehan, John Ray, Citizens National Bank
Mellin, Gilbert M., Whitney National Bank

Millen, Kenneth, Management Science America, Inc.
Miller, Christine C., University of Georgia
Morris, Robert E., IBM Corporation
Mourant, Roger R., Professional Bancorp
Murphy, Amy, Federal Reserve Bank of Atlanta
Murphy, William T., Murco Drilling Corporation
Neel, C. Warren, University of Tennessee
Nolan, Patrick, Hammer, Siler, George Associates
Oliver, Richard A., Federal Reserve Bank of Atlanta
Parker, Joel R., Federal Reserve Bank of Atlanta
Patrick, Joseph E., Jr., Label America, Inc.
Pattillo, Robert A., Pattillo Construction Company, Inc.
Peery, Charles L., The First National Bank of Florence
Perelman, Ellen, *Transition Magazine*
Pierce, Jeff S., Jr., First Federal Savings and Loan Association
Pisa, John C., Louisiana National Bank
Powers, Chris, Federal Reserve Bank of Atlanta
Presley, Charles B., First Railroad and Banking Company of Georgia
Quillian, Rudy T., Valuation Services of LaGrange
Rhodes, Nancy, Federal Reserve Bank of Atlanta
Rockoff, Lisa, Federal Reserve Bank of Atlanta
Rosenbaum, Mary, Federal Reserve Bank of Atlanta
Ross, Paul H., First National Bank of Chatsworth
Runyon, Marvin, Nissan U.S.A.
Russell, James, *The Miami Herald*
Savage, John, Nucor Corporation
Searle, Philip F., Sun Banks, Inc.
Shaw, James W., First City Federal Savings and Loan Association
Shoffner, Robert M., First Bank of Savannah
Shulman, Warren S., Garrett and Lane Color Laboratory
Smallwood, Jim L., First National Bank (Panama City)
Smith, H. Terry, Federal Reserve Bank of Atlanta
Smithers, J. Michael, First Federal Savings Bank
Steinhauser, Delores W., Federal Reserve Bank of Atlanta
Strickland, Robert, Trust Company of Georgia
Sullivan, Gene D., Federal Reserve Bank of Atlanta
Swint, A. G., Acme Engineering Company
Tapp, Gary, Federal Reserve Bank of Atlanta
Taylor, Edwina, Federal Reserve Bank of Atlanta
Tucker, Thomas J., AmSouth Bank, N.A.
Uceda, Gus, Federal Reserve Bank of Atlanta
Vincent, Carolyn H., Federal Reserve Bank of Atlanta
Walker, Tom, *The Atlanta Journal*
Wall, Larry D., Federal Reserve Bank of Atlanta

Wallace, John M., Federal Reserve Bank of Atlanta
Watson, Robinson R., Tennessee Valley Authority
Watts, Gibbs H., First National Bank of Dalton
Watts, James A., Deloitte, Haskins & Sells
Weberman, Ben, *Forbes*
Weiss, James A., Citicorp Acceptance Company
Wells, Joel R., Jr., Sun Banks, Inc.
Whigham, Pamela V., Federal Reserve Bank of Atlanta
Whitehead, David D., Federal Reserve Bank of Atlanta
Williams, Mary L., Widener University
Wilson, J. Miles H., Simons Eastern Company
Wilson, W. Gene, Federal Reserve Bank of Atlanta
Wood, C. Martin, III, Flowers Industries, Inc.
Woodard, George D., First American Corporation
Wright, Dennis L., Mosler Safe Company
Yellowless, Robert A., American Telesystems Corporation
Young, Alan, Office of the Comptroller of the Currency

Selected Bibliography

Abernathy, W. J. "Competitive Decline in U.S. Innovation: The Management Factor." *Research Management* 25 (Sept. 1982): 34–41.

Abernathy, William J., Kim B. Clark, and Alan M. Kantrow. " 'Mature' Industries Can Be Revitalized." *Research Management* 26 (July–Aug. 1983): 6–7.

————. "The New Industrial Competition." *Harvard Business Review* 59 (Sept.–Oct. 1981): 68–81.

"American Steel: Resurrection [Nucor Corp.]." *Economist*, Apr. 2, 1983, pp. 75–76.

Bernstein, A. "Making Dough [Flowers Industries]." *Forbes*, Apr. 25, 1983, pp. 60 +.

Brinkerhoff, Derick W., and Rosabeth Moss Kanter. "Appraising the Performance of Performance Appraisal." *Sloan Management Review* 21 (Spring 1980): 3–16.

Cook, J. "We Started from Ground Zero [Nissan]." *Forbes*, Mar. 12, 1984, pp. 98–101 +.

Eickhoff, M. Kathryn. "Inflation versus Political Freedom." *Business Economics* 17 (Jan. 1982): 17–20.

————. "Plant vs. Equipment Considerations in the Capital Goods Outlook." *Business Economics* 12 (Sept. 1977): 50–54.

Gissen, J. "Do One Thing and Do It Well [Charter Medical Corp.]." *Forbes*, Dec. 5, 1983, pp. 153–54.

Imlay, John P., Jr. "Growing Importance of Computer Services." *Office* 89 (Jan. 1979): 158–60.

Kanter, Rosabeth Moss. "The American Corporate Renaissance." *Directors and Boards* 8 (Winter 1984): 38–42.

————. "The Change Masters: How People and Companies Succeed in the New Corporate Era." *National Association of Bank Women Journal* 59 (July–Aug. 1983): 4–8.

————. *The Change Masters: Innovation for Productivity in the American Corporation.* New York: Simon and Schuster, 1983.

————. "Climbing the Pyramid Alone." *Wharton Magazine* 2 (Fall 1977): 38–44.

———. "Dilemmas of Managing Participation." *Organizational Dynamics* 11 (Summer 1982): 5–27.

———. "Frontiers for Strategic Human Resource Planning and Management." *Human Resource Management* 22 (Spring–Summer 1983): 9–21.

———. "Life at the Top." *Canadian Banker and ICB Review* 88 (Oct. 1981): 51–55.

———. "The Middle Manager as Innovator." *Harvard Business Review* 60 (July–Aug. 1982): 95–105.

———. "Power Failure in Management Circuits." *Harvard Business Review* 57 (July–Aug. 1979): 65–75.

———. "Power Games in the Corporation." *Psychology Today* 11 (July 1977): 48–53 + .

———. *Work and Family in the United States: A Critical Review and Agenda for Research and Policy.* New York: Russell Sage Foundation, 1977.

———, and Barry A. Stein. "Birth of a Saleswoman." *Across the Board* 16 (June 1979): 14–24.

———, with Barry A. Stein. *A Tale of "O": On Being Different in an Organization.* New York: Harper and Row, 1980.

Kantrow, Alan M. "The Political Realities of Industrial Policy." *Harvard Business Review* 61 (Sept.–Oct. 1983): 76–86.

———. "The Strategy-Technology Connection." *Harvard Business Review* 58 (July–Aug. 1980): 6–21.

———. "The Sun Also Rises for Sunset Industries." *Across the Board* 20 (May 1983): 48–54.

———. "Why Read Peter Drucker?" *Harvard Business Review* 58 (Jan.–Feb. 1980): 74–82.

Kotter, J. P. "What Effective General Managers Really Do." *Harvard Business Review* 60 (Nov.–Dec. 1982): 156–67.

Lawrence, Paul R., and Davis Dyer. *Renewing American Industry.* New York: Free Press, 1983.

"Leader of the Pack [J. Wells of Sun Banks]." *Forbes,* Mar. 12, 1984, p. 150.

Martin, Preston. "Q: Who Will Be the Future Players in the Market?" *Savings Institutions* 105 (Jan. 1984): S12–13.

———. "Restructuring the Banking Industry: Is There a Need?" *Independent Banker* 32 (Dec. 1982): 17–19 + .

Reich, Robert B. *The Next American Frontier.* New York: Times Books, 1983.

Rosenbloom, Richard S., and Alan M. Kantrow. "The Nurturing of Corporate Research." *Harvard Business Review* 60 (Jan.–Feb. 1982): 115–23.

Savage, John. "Incentive Programs at Nucor Corporation Boost Productivity." *Personnel Administrator* 26 (Aug. 1981): 33–36 + .

Stein, Barry A., and Rosabeth Moss Kanter. "Permanent Quality of Work Life." *Journal of Applied Behavioral Science* 16 (July–Sept. 1980): 371–88.

Wells, Joel R., Jr. "Changes Challenge Florida's Financial Institutions." *Business and Economic Dimensions* 17, no. 2 (1981): 2–4.

Index